THE FISH
IN MY LIFE

Also by George Lassalle

The Adventurous Fish Cook

Chasing the Chattel

**Sainsbury Classic Cookbooks:
Fish and Shellfish**

THE FISH
IN MY LIFE

*Cooking and eating fish
for health and happiness*

GEORGE LASSALLE

*Illustrated by
Harriet Lassalle*

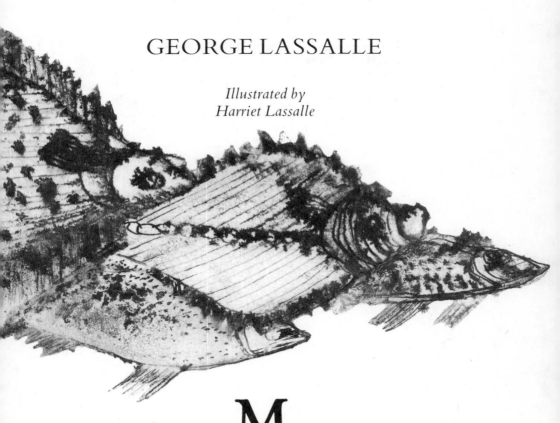

M
MACMILLAN
LONDON

First published 1989 by
MACMILLAN LONDON LIMITED
4 Little Essex Street London WC2R 3LF
and Basingstoke

Associated companies in Auckland, Delhi, Dublin, Gaborone,
Hamburg, Harare, Hong Kong, Johannesburg, Kuala Lumpur,
Lagos, Manzini, Melbourne, Mexico City, Nairobi, New York,
Singapore and Tokyo

A CIP catalogue record for this book is available from the
British Library

ISBN 0–333–49942–5

Typeset by Bookworm Typesetting, Manchester.

Printed in Hong Kong

For Caroline

CONTENTS

ACKNOWLEDGEMENTS

To Soraya Antonius for *Samak Harra*

To Leonard Bloom for *Bloom's Baroque Pickled Fish*

To Edna Uys for information

To Androula Costi, ‘Βασίλισσα της Κουζίνας για τα ωραία παραδοσιακά Κυπριώτικα της φαγητά

To Maroula Zenonos, authority on Cypriot life and language

To Meric Dobson, for his culinary skills and his wide knowledge of cuisinological lore

To Kyle Cathie for constant encouragement, unfailing help

1
A FISHY LIFE

When I first sat down to plan this book, I suddenly found myself swaying in my chair, and from upstairs came a sharp sound of falling objects. 'An earthquake?' I wondered. 'What an omen!' In the library, where I was sitting, my desk started to move away from me, and to confirm my surmise, *Mary Queen of Scots*, a massive leather-bound volume, slipped from its shelf and fell to the floor with a disconcerting thud. I noted the date and time: 8 November 1987; 10.00 am (Cyprus time).

At the very start of a new enterprise, this surely must have some special meaning for me, I thought, and it was not long before my rationalising human mind had found a happy interpretation of the omen. Forty-three years ago I had experienced, at this same time of year, a similar seismic shock in Istanbul. On that occasion, in 1944, it had been the middle of the night, and the denizens of the street where I was living had poured out on to the cobbles, ululating to their several gods, prophets and saints in ecumenical cacophony. That tremor, too, had been very mild (4.5 on the

Richter Scale), but only a few days later I had wangled an irregular posting, via Cairo, to Greece, where I arrived in time for a thrilling Christmas – Athens was then under seige by communist guerrillas – at the Grande Bretagne Hotel. This Cyprus tremor could therefore, I argued, only presage for me further happy adventures – but this time in the world of fish and fish cookery.

My motives in writing this book are much the same as those which impelled me to write *The Adventurous Fish Cook*. I want to impart to others some of the satisfactions and pleasures in the cooking and eating of fish that I have enjoyed in the course of an already long life in which I have become, as one critic of the previous book put it, 'a fanatic obsessed with his pop-eyed subject'.

In the Introduction to that book I rather illogically attributed the growth of my obsession to the impact on my mind of two marvellous experiences, ten years apart, connected with fishing: the first in Ireland, on Lough Corrib, the second in the narrow waters between Euboea and Boetia in Greece, where I was staying as a guest of a lovable eccentric, Francis Turville-Petre, on the lovely islet of Aghios Nikolaos where he had built a strange bungalow. It was here that I began to learn to cook, guided, to begin with, only by a battered *Mrs Beeton* and assisted by a village boy.

I should have realised, when I wrote that Introduction, that obsessions do not suddenly descend on one, like Pauline conversions, and that mine could not be fully accounted for by just two – admittedly powerful – experiences undergone at an interval of ten years. Obsessions are the result of slow accumulating growth, seeded early in life when the mind is at its most receptive. Searching back through my early memories I soon gathered a wealth of evidence to demonstrate the initial planting of the seed, the early growth and later development of my benign mania.

Back, then, to the year 1919, when I was eight years old and about to leave Holy Trinity Convent in Bromley, Kent, where my parents had put me out of harm's way for the duration of the First World War. I remember in vivid detail those happy years spent in the care of a Belgian order of refugee nuns, and can find no trace there of any fishy influence. That was to come with my transfer to a prep school at the Benedictine Priory in Ealing. It was from there that my mother, now for the first time released from her wartime work, was able to take us children to the seaside for prolonged summer holidays. What prompted her to choose the village of Kingsdown I shall never know, but she must have been divinely inspired. Kingsdown was at that time (I dare not hope it still is) a gloriously unsmart fishing village consisting of two short, cottage-lined streets tucked in under the eastern edge of the white cliffs of Dover. It boasted a lifeboat which was frequently called out in rough weather. The volunteer crew were all expert hereditary fishermen and men of the sea whose names have been current in these parts since the days of the Romans: Jarvis, Arnold, Pittock, Sutton, Bingham, Hoskins – names to figure in romantic fiction about pirates, smugglers, revenue men . . .

Our holiday cottage was at the seaward end of North Street. Our landlady was a Mrs Bingham, a fisherman's widow, who shopped, cooked, swept, cleaned and laundered for us throughout our stay. In order to make it possible for her to carry out her heavy housekeeping chores, we would disappear from her cottage after breakfast and spend the day in a large wind-and-rain-proof hut on the beach. In fine weather this large hut could be opened up to allow us sheltered sunbathing though, at such times, we would be more likely to be rushing about on the sands, perhaps shrimping if the tide was out, which was always rewarding, or fishing from a breakwater with our hand-lines and weighted paternosters hurled out a pitiable distance into the sea for a meagre catch of eels we never liked to handle; or perhaps we would be lending our puny strength to the stalwarts turning the big capstan, to haul up, on greased railway sleepers, a boat just in from fishing, when would come the thrilling inspection of the catch: mostly cod, codling, plaice, dabs, a conger and some fair-sized crabs – a lovely motley to behold. Part of the catch would be weighed and bagged for me to take to Mrs Bingham with a note of the amount charged to her account. This was an errand after my own heart, and I would often find Mrs Bingham busy in her kitchen, from which there always emanated the heady mouth-watering scent of a fish stock or soup in the making. These stolen nasal gratifications have since returned to me vividly at intervals throughout my life.

Out fishing with hand-lines was never very satisfying, but we made up for this shortcoming by what we saw as our brilliant performance when we went prawning in the rocky area under the tall cliffs between Kingsdown and St Margaret's Bay. The area was not always open to us, part of it being used as a firing range by the War Department. When this happened, red flags were flown, indicating the danger zone: the rocks below which were then strictly out of bounds. The range, however, was not much used and we could count on prawning in deep rock pools for most of the summer.

Prawning is not a pastime for the impatient, the clumsy, or the noisy fidget. The weapons with which these Lilliputian contests are fought are of the simplest: a wide-based inverted conical net, weighted at its narrower end, and at its wide-open mouth attached by strings to a large chunk of cork to keep the whole thing afloat; a stout forked stick, to be inserted under the cork so that the net, when observed to be full of prey, can be suddenly snatched up out of the water, thus preventing the escape of a very active and athletic adversary. The prawn likes his bait to be highly *faisandé*, and as he has cannibalistic appetites the lure to offer him is another – but very unfresh – prawn. You should cut up this decaying prawn and impale its almost phosphorescent pieces on a narrow wooden skewer and, from the top of the net, place it well down towards the bottom, so that each end is well held by the mesh. Now shop around for a wide, deep, sandy-bottomed rock pool, and drop your net into it. The only things not now completely immersed in water are the supporting strings and the chunk of cork that keeps the net open, at its wide end, to customers. At the same time (and this is perhaps the most important of the tactical rules of the game) push the fork of your stick well under the chunk of cork, and let the stick lie on the rock beside you within easy reach of both your hands, ready to snatch up and out at the critical moment. Down on your hunkers now, facing the sun so that no part of you throws a shadow on the pool. Tell your sister to stop singing that mindless end-of-term convent song in praise of Mother Aloysia, and in complete silence wait, watch, and pray.

When you drop your net into the deep sandy bottom of the pool, every living thing in it will instantly vanish. After perhaps fifteen minutes of complete stillness and silence the pool's denizens will begin to reappear, nervously at first and with extreme caution, so that the slightest of coughs or any brusque movement will send them racing back to cover, in sand or rock crevice. Another fifteen minutes, and by now the corrupt savours of your bait will have begun to penetrate through the pool and excite your prey to venture into the wide-open top of the net and sink down eagerly to the loaded skewer at the bottom, beginning to nibble competitively at the fragrant meal. But now you will find that there are other predators about – apart from yourself. A sudden puff of sand from the bottom of the pool will disclose the presence of a not-so-small crab with sharp cutting claws, which, if it finds its way into the net, is quite capable of damaging your catch and making off with the bait.

PRAWN OR SHRIMP NET, AND PRAWN POTS

The prawner's moment of decision has come. He should not be too greedy. If he has identified the presence of two or three prawns at work on the bait, he should then strike smartly upwards with his forked stick before the crab has found its way into the net. Two or three prawns seem a meagre catch for a half-hour's anxious watch, but there are another three hours of prawning ahead and, by the time you go home, you will probably have, between you, some dozen medium-sized prawns: quite enough for one of Mrs Bingham's prawn salads, to supplement the two large crabs she has dressed for high tea . . .

Yes, it is clear to me now that it was at Kingsdown that the first seeds were planted and began to germinate. It was not only the marvellous meals of fresh fish provided by Mrs Bingham in North Cottage which had an effect on me; the whole village simply reeked of the sea and fish and fishy gear and fishermen. There was the smell of tar, glue, tarpaulin jackets, kippers and bloaters smoking in the pub across the road from North Cottage, the smell of the grease on the capstans and railway sleepers from which the fishing boats were launched or drawn up on to the beach. And over all, as some kind of theme song, was the ominous wailing of the foghorns from the lightships on the Goodwin Sands, not so distant it seemed in the often foggy nights and mornings. This whole atmosphere seemed to focus and to chime in with those other sounds of grinding heavy feet on the gravel road and the noise of the heavy fortnightly dray from Fremlins, come to supply the Trafalgar pub and the Marquis of Zetland Arms and perhaps bringing, as a favour, one sack of coals for Mr Pittock, the mini-supermarket of his time, provider of all things, under the broad label of grocer.

Two summer holidays later, I found myself more in love with Kingsdown than ever, but when this holiday ended, the time had come for me to move up into the mainstream of educational life in the Priory School proper, where the usual hurdles of examinations stretched before me: Junior Cert, School Cert, and Higher Cert. Though the Priory was a very small school, the Benedictines took the education of their charges seriously. I myself sat for each of the above-mentioned exams twice over, and passed with Distinction marks in one subject or another each time. A nasty, successful little swot and, with my conspicuous devotion to my religious duties, a sanctimonious prig I certainly was – and proud of it, moreover, at the time. Somehow, the cult of fish I was nursing in my mind had become mixed up with my religious beliefs, and this gave me a feeling of apartness from my schoolfellows.

Events were now to prove that, in moving from my last holiday in Kingsdown directly to my first term at the Priory School proper, I was simply moving from one sphere of fishy influence into another, that other being Dom Cyril Rylance OSB.

Father Cyril was in charge of French Studies and was also choirmaster. As I was in his class and also in the choir, we saw each other pretty well every day, and I became a self-appointed fetcher and carrier of musical scores. It was not long before his interest in fish and his passion for angling showed themselves. I

6

would sometimes catch him polishing and playing with his rods, studying maps and timetables, and so on. At such times he was obviously totally absorbed in his memories, and his voice was soft and almost musical. Not so in the classroom where, if anyone made a stupid mistake in French syntax, he would bellow his simulated rage in a voice which could be heard in Ealing Broadway, at least a mile from the classroom. This propensity for yelling at his pupils made him, oddly enough, one of the more popular masters in the school, and this popularity was greatly increased when it was discovered that Father Cyril was the fastest celebrant of the early-morning Mass, habitually reaching his final *'Ite, missa est'* within fifteen minutes of his opening *'Introibo'*.

One day, when I was delivering a batch of musical scores to his study, I saw a large map of the West of England laid out on his flat-topped desk. Perceiving my interest in the map, Father Cyril said, 'I'm planning my Easter holiday. Ten days' trout and salmon fishing from Ross-on-Wye.' And then, 'Ever done any fishing, boy?' he asked.

'Very little,' I replied. 'Only by the seaside with a hand-line. I do like *prawning*, though. I had some very good catches, prawning last summer.'

'Where was that?' he inquired.

'At Kingsdown in Kent,' I said, proud to name the emotional epicentre of my personal fish cult.

Brushing my meagre experience aside, he then asked, 'Would you like to learn, boy?'

Eagerly I replied, 'Oh yes, indeed, Father. Very much.'

'The art of real fishing, I mean. The noble art of angling. It will be a long time before you're any good, but I could teach you the elements, to start you off. Do you like fish, boy?'

'Oh yes. I *love* fish.'

'To eat, I mean. We've the choir treat coming next term and we can all feast on Scots salmon then. Would you like to come with me to Ross, as my server at daily Mass? It might be arranged. I can tell you now you'll be top of the French class again this term. And you've worked very hard in the choir. Of course, I shall have to meet your parents first, and get their approval. Don't count on it, boy, but I'll have a try.'

I wrote home that evening, stressing my love of fish and fishing, and the splendour of this opportunity to learn angling from an expert, without having to buy any equipment of my own. My father, a perfervid Roman Catholic who was, some time later, to become a member of the Third Order of St Francis, met Father Cyril, and the two got on well together. They shared common ground, my father being himself a talented amateur musician who had composed many short polyphonic motets, some of which the school choir at a later date performed.

My father wrote to the Headmaster and the Prior, and a consensus was reached that, in view of the high standard of my work in school and choir, I should be allowed this special ten-day holiday as Father Cyril's official acolyte.

Thus, then – although that first expedition was to prove a fiasco owing to the weather – at an early stage of my schooldays did the two most powerful influences and arbiters of my future come together to nurture in me the cult of fish, which I now felt had been officially sanctioned by Church and State; the latter as represented by paternal authority.

Although the flooding of the Wye and continual rainstorms washed out all plans to fish from Ross, Father Cyril's acute disappointment seemed to be more on my account than his own. Had he not undertaken to initiate me into the mysteries of angling? At least he could instruct me in such rudiments of the game as how to tie a fly.

'You should, of course, make your own flies,' he said. 'But my left hand is arthritic and it's a very difficult job for me. So I use artificial, ready-made flies, some of which work very well indeed. It still needs a very delicate touch just to tie the fly on. Watch carefully, boy.' And he showed me how to attach the fly and tie the special knot which would hold the hook concealed and prevent the fish tearing the fly from the line without being caught on it.

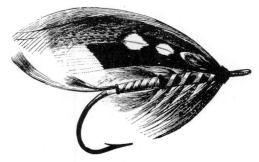

Dull work I found this, but I persevered, and suddenly my reward came: for the first time in my life I was to be given a demonstration of imaginative mime, or what I would refer to now as 'creative nostalgia'.

The wind had suddenly dropped. A dim sun was just beginning to glimmer in the sky. The modest lodging-house where we were staying had a big lawn, pockmarked with plantains and patches of daisies. 'Come on, boy,' said Father Cyril. 'Let's try some casting. That daisy patch over there by the edge of the lawn – that's my fish.' And with a splendidly nonchalant elegance and vigour combined, he began using the rod like a whip, held in his right hand, and at each stroke of the whip, with his left hand, drawing out line from the reel which produced the sharp, purring music of a well-oiled ratchet.

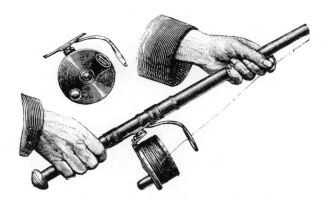

It took him four whiplash casts, increasing the range after each of the first three, to bring his fly exactly over the daisy patch, letting the fly at last seemingly hover over the flowers and then settle plumb in the middle.

This splendid little show thrilled me. As I watched, a transformation came over Father Cyril's countenance. His skin took on a rosier hue, and he appeared to have grown suddenly younger as, again and again, choosing a distant target on the lawn, he repeated his magical act for my edification and his own manifest pleasure.

'Your turn, boy.' And as he handed me his trout-rod he was grinning wildly, just another schoolboy, as pleased with his

prowess as I was disappointed by my own lamentable performance. But, as a fishing expedition, our holiday could not, I
thought, be considered a total failure. For on that lawn I had seen
not the daisy patch, as Father Cyril had, but – real fish.

Although we returned to the Priory, and then I to my home, not
exactly as conquering heroes, our keenness to plan another sortie
was unblunted. Already Father Cyril had picked a scene for
exploits which might make up for our recent disaster and restore
my confidence. Connemara was to be the setting for our next
adventure, and a month was set aside out of the long summer
holiday when it was unlikely to rain more than half the time,
though the uncertainties of the Irish weather were well known.
We would lodge in a village called Twelve Crows Nest, on the
shores of Lough Corrib, and go after the brown trout for which
that lake is justly famous. Meanwhile, as this planning went
ahead, we were in the middle of the summer term, and Father
Cyril's choir treat was upon us.

This annual event was a generous reward for the voluntary
services of twelve of us boys who practised and sang our way
valiantly through a variable number of polyphonic – chiefly Early
English – Masses in the course of a year. Byrd, Tye, Tallis,
Taverner – and even Palestrina – were in our repertoire, and we
had a choir standard which was beginning to draw favourable
attention from Westminster Cathedral Choir whose director, Sir
Richard Terry, would occasionally appear to monitor our
progress.

The choir treat was as exciting as Father Cyril, with limited
resources, could make it, and traditionally it included in its
culminating event, which was a picnic, a giant Scotch salmon
and a monster salad befitting it. Our departure was watched by
envious unprivileged boys. We mounted the steps of a large
horse-drawn brake, fitted with bench seats, and helped to load on
the crates containing our eagerly awaited banquet. Every choirboy
was handed a generous tip, and our hearts were high as the heavy
equipage jolted through the gates of the school and set off on its
way to Burnham Beeches. Here, Father Cyril and his staff – a
junior monk and a kitchen hand or two – would immediately start
the preparations for the meal, putting up a trestle table, laying a
cloth, setting it with knives and forks and plates, and displaying –
though discreetly, under a large gauze-wire cover to keep flies

away – the gorgeous great fish which I, at least, would be tasting for the first time.

A large handbell summoned us to the table – well away from the toffee-apple and ice-cream booths scattered about the paths away from the woods – and Father Cyril called us up, one by one. Each of us was given a generous portion of the noble fish, which was probably larger than any he himself had ever caught (but whose match, I could see him thinking, might be met with, hooked, gaffed and netted, and hauled into the boat we would have at our disposal on Corrib later that summer).

It was delicious, and the mayonnaise real, not from a bottle. The salad – of hard-boiled eggs and potatoes, cucumber, watercress, tomatoes – was likewise specially dressed in what I would come to know later as a vinaigrette.

Of our triumphal visit to Connemara and Achill Island later that summer, I have already written in the Introduction to *The Adventurous Fish Cook* and I will not enlarge on it here. I shall only say that, although my introduction to salmon, at Burnham Beeches, can be assumed to have been an important staging-post in my gathering obsession, it did not have the mind-blowing effect experienced, later that summer, with the Lough Corrib brown trout. Probably this was because the trout had been personally caught by myself, and eaten within minutes of having been taken from the water, while the choir-outing salmon had undergone a long journey, packed in broken ice, by train from somewhere near Fort Augustus in Scotland.

As I leave the Priory and move to Worcester College, Oxford, I feel it a duty to offer a further note on Dom Cyril Rylance (R.I.P.). Although I was perhaps unaware of it at the time, he was one of the people who had a fundamental influence on my future life. When I eventually came to read Izaak Walton's *The Compleat Angler*, I recognised Dom Cyril at once as a fellow practitioner of that creative and imaginative nostalgia, and a fellow devotee of the simple, pastoral, sporting life by which the kinetic and cerebral elements of my regimen have partly been inspired. What John Buchan said of Walton, in his Introduction to the World's Classics edition of *The Compleat Angler*, may appropriately also be said of Father Cyril: 'Hence comes the angler – the sportsman, I love to think, who can feel all the old primeval excitement of his sport, and yet the man of culture to whom nature is more than a chalk-stream or a salmon-river, who has ears for Coridon's song as well as the plash of trout below the willows.'

Worcester College proved to be another potent centre of fishy influence. The college buttery and kitchens, under the expert direction of Mr Drake, the butler, were widely known as the best source in Oxford of delicious lunchtime lobster and salmon salads. In both these delicacies I indulged myself to the full. But it was outside the college that I first encountered – and formed an expensive taste for – oysters.

Oysters are a subject on which I must yield to a compulsion to digress. I shall always maintain the view that they are best taken *au naturel*: that is, opened and served in the deep shell with their juices. Although, in earlier years, I used to season them with a little red pepper or a *soupçon* of hot sauce, age has made me chaste, and I now like only a few drops of lemon juice. All the same, if you are serving forth a feast of oysters, you should also supply (in addition, of course, to the obligatory crustless, finely sliced brown bread and butter) cayenne pepper and Tabasco sauce. (This raises the question of how many oysters you should provide for each person. Even nowadays I would say that if you are having nothing but oysters, a dozen is essential. However, as a first course, six is perfectly adequate.)

I was not – alas! – alive at the time when oysters were known as 'the poor man's food'. In those days, cooks (and cookery writers) made use of them with reckless abandon. The extraordinary adaptability of oysters enabled them to be employed in ways which would not be possible with any other form of seafood. *Mrs Beeton* (I am referring to my favourite 1890 edition, of which more later), among sixteen oyster recipes, gives prescriptions for Oyster Forcemeat – for roast or boiled turkey – Oyster Ketchup, and Oyster Sausages in which they are combined with minced veal.

This last recipe makes me feel very nervous. I have always found the combination of seafood and meat displeasing (just as the inclusion of chicken and eggs in the same dish is an abhorrent idea to me). From this *diktat* I exclude the noble paella and, though with personal reservations, the traditional association of fish with bacon (see page 92). By the way, oysters can be 'kebabed' with bacon in a similar fashion to scallops, though I myself would not treat them in this way. All the same, proving a total lack of logic, Angels on Horseback (page 102) is my favourite savoury.

Nowadays the oysters-and-meat relationship survives, as far as I am aware, largely in two beef recipes. (Beef! What other seafood has ever entered into such an – unholy? – alliance?) First is the steak-and-kidney pudding (*never* pie) where there is an old tradition of the inclusion of a few oysters. This is still respectfully adhered to by modern cookery writers, and still followed in one or two expensive 'eating-houses' of the Olde English type. I find I have no particular objection to it. Second is the Carpetbag Steak (vulgar by name as by nature) where a thick outer integument of beef confines a huddle of the unhappy bivalves. Against this I set my face, as I do against the presence of oysters with lamb chops in a glorified Lancashire hotpot about which I read recently.

In my own choice of cooked oyster dishes, no such relationships are established. Proudly the oyster maintains its individual integrity.

FRIED OYSTERS

I cannot include this recipe without voicing my objection to 'battering'! Wipe the raw oysters and then egg-and-breadcrumb them, before quickly cooking them in clarified butter (see page 167). It is often recommended that fried oysters should be accompanied by tomato sauce (I must specify, in view of a reminiscence which follows shortly, that I do not mean tomato ketchup). I think this is a mistake, and that a lemon quarter is the ideal companion.

GRILLED OYSTERS WITH PARMESAN

This is a rich and splendid way of gilding the lily. Large oysters are best for it and, in this single instance, I would say that three would be sufficient for each person. I also prefer to eat this dish with crisp, hot, unbuttered toast, rather than the usual brown bread and butter.

oysters

1 dessertspoon double cream
for each oyster

ground black pepper

grated Parmesan cheese

melted butter

Open the oysters. Discard the upper shell and then cut the muscle which attaches the oyster to the lower one. Pour a spoonful of cream over each oyster, and add a pinch of finely ground black pepper. Sprinkle with Parmesan, and then pour on a very little melted butter. Place under a hot grill for 3–4 minutes.

OYSTER STEW

The two words in the title of this recipe seem to me to point each other up in a piquant manner. The oyster nowadays has such a purpureal aura of luxury, and stews (though so many are delicious as well as nourishing) have overtones of economy and 'making the best' of modest ingredients. The result is an opportunity to be gloriously lavish without (apparent) ostentation.

Obviously you will not use 'Whitstable Natives' for this recipe. The Portuguese variety is perfectly suitable . . . as are other cheaper, smaller oysters.

Unlike the two previous recipes, this one is definitely for a main course, and should satisfy four hungry people when accompanied by chunks of fresh crusty white bread. (The Americans eat oyster stews with hard crackers. British authors tend to 'garnish' them with fried *croûtons* or with snippets of toasted bread. Neither of these alternatives appeals to me.)

---

3 dozen oysters

300ml (½ pint) double cream

100g (4oz) butter

---

a good pinch of cayenne pepper

½ teaspoon salt

---

a pinch of powdered mace

---

for garnish

1 dessertspoon parsley, finely chopped

Open the oysters and carefully pour off their juices into a pan. Remove the oysters from their shells. Bring the juices to a boil, and then simmer the oysters in this liquid until they 'plump out' and their edges curl (about 5 minutes). Strain the juices through a fine sieve into a jug. Keep the oysters warm in a serving-dish. Now amalgamate the cream, butter and seasonings on a very low heat. In no circumstances allow to boil. Slowly add the oyster juices to this mixture, while stirring constantly. Pour the resulting sauce over the oysters, mixing it in with a fork. Serve immediately, with a sprinkling of parsley.

Note: Until recently – very recently – I was possessed by the notion that the original recipe for the famous 'Prairie Oyster' morning-after remedy (a whole raw fresh egg, swallowed with the aid of a teaspoonful of Worcester Sauce, salt, pepper. and a drop of Tabasco sauce) contained an actual oyster instead of an egg.

I now find that this is not the case. It is, in fact, nonsense. How did such an illusion arise? Possibly as a result of a repressed craving for the 'real thing'? I often brood on the Vicomte de Mauduit's fascinating assertion, in his book *The Vicomte in the Kitchen*, that oysters are 'said to cure cretinism'.

I was introduced to oysters by one Horace Titus, the son of Helena Rubinstein. Horace was a dark, heavily built sophisticate of considerable, if sinister, charm, steeped in a Parisian cynicism which matched well with my own disillusionment at that time. It was from Horace that I had received my blue-paper-bound copy of *Ulysses*, the possession of which, in those innocent days, was a kind of certificate of depravity. I had entertained him once or twice in 'Wuggins', as Worcester College was then universally known, and in return he would ask me to dine at the George Grill and Restaurant, resort of better-off undergraduates. There we would invariably order oysters, and Horace would pay. These indulgences became a habit, Horace swopping his oyster-feasts for luncheons in 'Wuggins'.

I select one oyster-feast and its sequel to describe here, because it was that unexpected sequel which led directly to my subsequent sojourn on the Greek island where I began to cook.

Horace, as a self-professed *bon viveur* and voluptuary, had a strange way with oysters. He would fork his oyster, with its juices, out into a tablespoon, which he then filled with Heinz tomato ketchup, and swallow the spoonful down with an unnerving and most audible gulp. On this particular evening we had both had several glasses of sherry, and Horace suggested we should find out, in friendly competition, just how many oysters we could consume in an evening. 'I will pay,' he said. I let him have his way, and we began.

Four dozen oysters and three bottles of ketchup later, Ehrsam, the proprietor, was worriedly checking his supplies of the latter. Poor Ehrsam, faced with a decision either to remove oysters from his regular menu, or tomato ketchup, normally supplied free to customers, was already in a very nervous condition: two Polish counts, at a table by the window, overlooking the Cornmarket, had reached that stage of celebration in which, after a toast or two in honour of some lamentable event in their country's tragic history, they would feel a compulsion to begin eating their wineglasses. At another table, an unpleasant group had been pressing Ehrsam to put through a call on the telephone to the Vatican where, they averred, the Holy Father was eagerly waiting to hear from them. This was a task he was reluctant and linguistically unqualified even to attempt to perform in the generally confused state of international communication at that time. Gloomily Ehrsam must have thought that they probably wouldn't even pay their bill.

Suddenly into Ehrsam's angst-ridden restaurant there now burst a group of tweedy young men led by one James Borthwick Dowdall of my college, owner of the most heavily tubed horse in the county, called Sailor, off which he fell every time he rode it.

'What's up?' I asked, reluctant to halt the even flow of oysters.

'Come on, George, you idle bugger. We're going to raid the Union, and we need two chaps to hold the fire-hose.'

This was the first I had heard of any such plan, but the idea of holding a hose on and possibly inundating the entire undergraduate political establishment, left, right and centre, at one go, had much to recommend it. I regarded all university politicians as being ambitious, self-advertising and enormously conceited. Horace, for whom the idea had just that spice of sacrilege which would attract him, murmured, 'What fun!'

'Come on then,' I said. 'You can be Number Two behind the spout. It's damned heavy and difficult to control.'

I suppose few people nowadays will remember or understand the furore created in the press at the time of the Union motion 'That this house will, in no circumstances, fight for King and Country'. (This was the year that Hitler came to power in Germany.) So Horace and I joined Dowdall and his band and we proceeded to the Union, where we took charge of the fire-hose, me at the business end, Horace behind me, helping to drag it through the doors and on to the floor of the House.

The members were a pathetic-looking lot as they cowered before my clumsy and dribbling weapon, which I swung round the debating hall in a decidedly menacing manner. While I did so, one of Dowdall's stalwarts walked smartly up to the Union's Indian Secretary, D. Karaka, snatched the minute-book from his table and, to murmurs of execration, tore out the offending motion and minute.

17

We withdrew with our prize and were led to rooms in Balliol where it was pinned to the panelled wall and photographed by a journalist. It was then cut up into several large pieces, jigsaw-fashion, and I came away with a generous portion of it. It was this portion which I took to Greece with me, that summer, and which won for me the freedom of the British colony in Athens.

There was a certain irony, by the way, in my next meeting with that Union Secretary, which occurred in wartime Cairo, 1942. I had occasion to call at the Ministry of Information, and was standing by the entrance desk, talking to a ravishing brunette who worked there, when who should walk up, in full military fig, but D. Karaka. When he saw me, his eyes came out on stalks. 'Do you two know each other?' asked the ravishing brunette (whose name, for future reference, was Elizabeth Gwynne). 'Captain Karaka, Lieutenant Lassalle.'

We shook hands.

How I came to arrive and settle for a time on the island of Aghios Nikolaos should, I think, also be told. On my finally coming down from Oxford – delayed not only by a term's rustication but by my changes from reading Forestry (my father's choice) to Law and eventually to Modern Languages – friends exerted themselves to find me a comfortable lodging and some kind of a job. For a time I stayed in Brompton Square, in a house owned by Val Goldsmith, a director of the BBC, whose roof also sheltered Denis Freeman, a BBC producer in the light entertainment field, and his fascinating sister, Irene. It was understood that I myself would eventually attain an established job in the BBC, and I was placed under Denis Freeman for training. A few one-line parts were thrown my way. However my vocal debut, as a gardener in Hyde Park, was not a notable success as all I had to do was repeatedly urge the rest of the cast: 'Oh, please do keep off the grass. Oh, please do keep off the grass.'

Meanwhile Irene, with whom I had fallen in love and had been having a passionate affair, was sent to a sanatorium in Montana Vermala, Switzerland, where it was hoped that her tendency to TB might be cured. We agreed that, at the end of her treatment, I should go out there and escort her home.

I could not have contemplated the expense involved in this gallant mission, had it not been for Holy Year, in which – for the encouragement of good English Catholic pilgrims – the third-class return fare had been reduced to only five pounds, a sum which even I could manage to raise in five minutes at the Café Royal. I could, on this ticket, break my journey in Milan, nip up to Montana, collect Irene and escort her home.

No arrival of eager lover to the rescue could ever have been less opportune for, at the sanatorium, I discovered that Irene was indeed packed and ready to leave; and also packed and ready to leave with her were the director of the sanatorium and another patient, the famous cricketer, Duleep Sinji, who had rented a villa in Stresa, on Lake Maggiore, for an 'extended convalescence' (a phrase I found so equivocal, in the circumstances, that I now present it to the editor of *Private Eye* for further use with discretion).

Bruised in heart and ego, I retraced my steps, via Milan, to Rome. I did not want to leave Europe. I still hoped for a summons from Irene who had promised that on completion of her 'convalescence' she would write to me, but my financial position made it impossible for me to hang about Rome, even in Holy Year. It now made sense to me that, in view of the enormously favourable exchange rate of the Greek drachma, I should move on to Greece, and I headed for Athens where I knew I would find two friends I had last seen in the Café Royal before I left.

In Athens I found there were two grades of English nationals. There was the usual number of expatriate worthies in business and, on a far dizzier plane, the diplomats and various drifting Oxford men and Old Etonians. Mention of those who were still there, or who had just left – 'yesterday, my dear!' – for Salzburg or Istanbul, sounds like a casting call for a rehearsal of *Brideshead Revisited*: Mark Ogilvie-Grant, Alistair Graham, Evelyn Waugh, Leonard Bower, Jim Tovey, Brian Howard, Terence Rattigan. It may have been Holy Year in Rome, but in Athens it was the Year of the Exquisites.

My own credentials consisted of my large segment of the offending Oxford Union motion and minute, on the strength of which I was immediately made a member of the small *recherché* luncheon club run by Captain Stewart Hay – a good cook, it should be noted – in his flat in the smart Kolonaki district. It was at my first lunch there that I met Francis Turville-Petre.

Very handsome, in a dark-browed, *Wuthering Heights* kind of way, Francis's strongly weathered face seemed to bear the marks

Francis Turville Petre with an uncertain and
dubious object, on Aghios Nikolaos.

of many martyrdoms of the spirit. Evidently of a highly nervous
temperament, he was apt to twitch and wring his hands in his lap
if too suddenly addressed. Up to that time I had not met anyone
whom the word 'eccentric' had been so clearly designed to
describe.

After studying Anthropology and Archaeology, Francis had
joined a dig on a site in Palestine under the aegis of an
Oxford-sponsored expedition. He very soon began to show an
independence of action which met with disapproval from those in
charge. Francis, however, went ahead in his eccentric way and
was lucky enough to discover – and excavate in a professional
manner – what is now known to prehistoric anthropologists as the
'Galilee skull' and which still holds an honourable place among
important discoveries in this field.

His differences with the authorities, however, continued (the
hectic quality of his private life can never have been helpful here),
and his official career was effectively ended. Later he joined
Magnus Hirschfeld – a pioneer expert on homosexuality and
campaigner for its legalisation – in research at Hirschfeld's
Instituut Für Sexual-Wissenschaft (Institute for Sexual Science) in
Berlin, and left shortly before the Institute and its library and
museum were destroyed by the Nazis.

When he moved to Aghios Nikolaos, he was initially attracted
by a tumulus on the mainland coast just opposite the island, which
he hoped to get permission to excavate from the continuingly

uncooperative authorities. Meanwhile he started to build the house which he had himself designed on the back of a cigarette packet, and where he entertained a remarkably various collection of visitors. When he invited me there, he mentioned that he had a couple of refugees from Berlin in residence. 'They're a bit fussy as guests but you won't see much of them. They keep themselves to themselves. In fact they're beginning to bore me. But do come if you can, and stay as long as you like. Come up and have a look at the island first.'

Francis was leaving for the island next day, as soon as Mitso, his chauffeur, had collected the car, which was in for repair. 'If you can be ready by nine in the morning,' he said, 'I'll pick you up at the Mistra.' (This was the hotel where I was staying.)

From Athens to Khalkis it was a run of about three hours of rough, rather hazardous mountain road, but it felt quite safe as Mitso never ventured to go as fast as forty miles an hour. The car was a Buick and, I should say, third- or fourth-hand at least, but Mitso controlled it well, and though Francis expected punctures we had none. Passing through the village of Khalia, on the way to the small bay of Aulis, Francis again mentioned his two refugees.

'Perhaps you know one of them – Isherwood?'

'No, I don't know him,' I said.

'He's written a book people think is promising. And there's his little German friend, of course. If you don't mind, I won't introduce you straight off when we land. Isherwood's sure to want to complain about something. But they'll probably be having their siesta. With any luck, we can slip by.'

Mitso, on reaching the beach, punched the car's hooter a couple of times, and almost at once two men could be seen getting into a boat in the small sheltering harbour of the island about a mile and a half away. A quarter of an hour later we were aboard with our bits and pieces, and being rowed quickly out to the island over crystal-clear water in which I could see many tempting fish, mostly grey mullet but of a fine size.

Francis saw me staring into the water and said, 'You'll enjoy the night-fishing if you're interested.'

'More than interested,' I said.

We made as little noise as possible, on landing, and crept up a steep path towards the top of a flat hill covered with building paraphernalia: bricks, sacks of cement, lengths of iron, and so on.

This was the site for the still-unfinished house Francis was building.

On our way up, we had passed a smallish bell tent, firmly closed, and from that direction now came the querulous sound of voices in dispute.

'Pay no attention to them,' said Francis. 'They're at it day and night.'

Whatever the quarrel, it was being conducted in German, I realised. Francis said, 'They're both out of the same Berlin gutter, you understand. Come and sit down.'

We drew up chairs at a table on the cement base of the all-round veranda that was planned. Francis then fetched a litre bottle of retsina and two glass tumblers into which he poured large measures. 'Welcome,' he said. When he saw me looking round at the general disorder, he added, 'Oh, in another week, the house, apart from the bathroom and the veranda walls, will be complete. The roof, as you can see' – he pointed upwards – 'is already in place.'

I looked up – and it was.

'In two weeks,' he said, 'you'll be better off here than in your Mistra Hotel.'

'Done!' I said, and after a second glass of wine I stood up and looked around me. Wonderful! I had not realised that I was surrounded on all sides by tremendous views – the view to the east, towards Mount Dirfys in Euboea, being particularly spectacular. Francis, I thought, must be the luckiest, happiest Englishman alive. It was a Shakespeare island.

More wine washed down an unsatisfactory meal of chunks of meat cooked in milk – the sauce thickened with prunes – which had been cooked, and was now unsteadily served, by a large, bloated German, introduced as Erwin Hansen. We were undisturbed by the guests from the bell tent, and I camped under the roof of the unfinished house that night. The next day I was put on a train by Mitso at a junction from which it was a short journey into Athens, and saw nothing of Francis's unwelcome guests from Berlin. I might have missed them altogether but for the fact that, about ten days later, they left the island for Athens, where Francis was to give them a farewell lunch at Costi's: arguably the best restaurant in the city and certainly the most expensive.

Isherwood makes no mention of this occasion in his 'slice of autobiography', *Christopher and His Kind*, recording a 'semi–secret' departure from the island 'just after sunset' and not remembering if he said goodbye to Francis.

I, however, who was present at the lunch, remember it well. Francis had asked me to join them. 'Do help me out,' he said. 'I've simply nothing to say to those two pathetic characters, and if there isn't someone there that Christopher doesn't know, there's bound to be a quarrel. I'm sure that, in front of a stranger, Christopher will be very careful to be on his best behaviour. He talks well . . . about himself, of course.'

The food was indeed splendid. Lobster salad, with a delicious variant of *tartare* – which had plenty of chopped *rocca*, green peppers and gherkins blended into it – was followed by a perfect *risotto milanese* in which, apart from the main ingredients, truffles and saffron had not been spared. And the Valpolicella accompanying the meal was a relief after all the retsina I had consumed recently. But if I had expected to learn anything of Isherwood's conversational powers, I was disappointed, as German was the only language in which the Master would deign to speak.

This I felt to be a deliberate snub, as did Francis, who said, 'Can we talk in English? George doesn't speak any German.'

'I don't see why,' said Isherwood. 'There are three of us who do. So we're in the majority.'

We finished our meal in mutually resentful silence. Francis immediately called for the bill, wrote a cheque for the amount due, and got up. As I rose from the table with him, he said loudly, 'What a despicable little runt you are, Isherwood,' and we walked out of Costi's without farewells being exchanged. I felt rather inclined to agree with Francis's verdict, especially when, twenty-nine years later, I read in Isherwood's *Down There on a Visit* his malicious travesty of his former benefactor, who had died during the war.

The next day I returned to the island with Francis to find the house indeed complete in almost every necessity. I settled into a room which had a movable frame of sandfly netting over the window, allowing me to sleep soundly without breathing in the fumes from a Japanese Katacoil on my bedside table. This was luxury indeed, beyond the resources of the Mistra Hotel to provide.

Francis, overjoyed with his splendid new home – its entrance adorned with a handsome yellow tile he had apparently stolen from an Early Egyptian site – was already making lists of potential guests who might come and those who might refuse. I tackled him at once about the fishing and about the standards of Erwin Hansen's cooking. He could certainly not invite guests to stay unless we could feed them decently, however simply.

He said, 'Fish any night you like, unless it looks stormy. You had better take Mitso, the first time. He's most reliable. I'll speak to him today. But the cooking is a bit of a problem. You see, Erwin has to cook for all the men and boys on the island, a rather variable number, I'm afraid. We can hardly expect him to change his old soldier's habits. He was in the German army as a physical-training instructor. Then he worked for the Siemens electric firm. After that, he was an odd-job-man at Hirschfeld's Institute. He's no Brillat-Savarin. Perhaps you could help him out a little . . . guide his untutored hand. He has only one he can use, you know. His arm was crippled in Berlin when a bar-boy hit him with a bottle. He's been unlucky, poor fellow.'

I said, 'I really don't know much about cooking, Francis.'

'But I've got the most wonderful cookery book.' He darted into the house, emerging a few minutes later with a battered volume which he handed to me. Bound in shredding blue cloth, it was an entrancing book, delightfully illustrated. It was called *Mrs Beeton's Every-Day Cookery*. An edition published in 1890, it was arranged in alphabetical order. (Despite its lavish use of ingredients totally unobtainable on the island, I would gain from it the rudiments of cooking method.)

This conversation took place early in the morning, and now Erwin appeared, carrying our breakfast tray of bacon and eggs and two big mugs of strong tea. As he put the tray down on the table with a bump, I realised that he was drunk. It was not yet eight o'clock.

The German way of making bacon and eggs *(Eier und Speck)* is that in practice throughout Germany, I believe. I have nothing against it. Small sections of good, fine-cut streaky bacon are put in a small pan on a gentle fire. As the bacon fat melts and begins to crinkle, fresh eggs are broken into the pan and, as soon as the egg white is firm, the meal is served (a small pan for each person) with bread, the latter being used to soak up the bacon juices left after the eggs are eaten.

Erwin's version of this simple formula consisted of inch-square lumps of the coarsest quality bacon I have ever seen, fried almost to burning. The three eggs he had broken into each small pan had cemented these lumps of unchewable bacon to the pan's bottom. The shrivelled yolks were unattainable under a tough glaze of egg white, and there were no juices to be sopped up with bread. This would never do for some of the exquisites whose names I had seen on Francis's list of possible guests.

The thought of fishing kept me from brooding too much on the sad prospect of a daily subjection to the vagaries and excesses of Erwin's cooking. We ate what the workmen ate, and I soon discovered that the boy, Yianni, who had been appointed as scullion to assist Erwin was, in fact, doing the cooking without much help from his master. This peasant food was excellent. Beans, lentils or other pulses were cooked with onion and tomatoes with, once a week, the addition of chunks of pork, mutton or goat. Olive oil and garlic were plentifully used, and herbs to flavour the dish grew wild all over the island: thyme, marjoram, rosemary and bay. I had a feeling that if we could set in train a regular supply of fish from the surrounding waters, we could, with Yianni's simple talents, learnt at his grandmother's knee, put up a brave show, should any of Francis's guests accept his invitation. The only problem was how to prevent Erwin from attempting the heavy and over-rich dishes of Prussian *haute cuisine*. Francis was keen not to hurt his feelings.

My excitement grew throughout the following day, as I watched Mitso fixing the acetylene lamp, with its large reflecting shade, at the prow of the smaller of the two boats in the harbour. At about nine o'clock, after a supper of olives, slices of local sausage, bread and cheese, washed down by plenty of retsina, Mitso and I went aboard and, once outside the little harbour, he started up the small outboard engine and we fizzed away. There was only a sickle moon, but a brilliant display of stars made it seem like daylight. We moved steadily towards the headland around which a wide course must be steered to reach Khalkis on the mainland. Suddenly there was a bright flash which lit up the scene theatrically. This was followed within seconds by the boom of an explosion.

Mitso was no less excited than I was as he opened the throttle of the outboard and began to round the headland. '*Tha fame psari avrio!*' ('Tomorrow we shall have fish!') he almost yelled. Ahead, a dark shape showing no lights was moving away from us fast. Illegal dynamiters of fish, hearing our small engine probably magnified by echoes from the headland, had thought that we were the fishing patrol, intent on arresting them.

Suddenly we found ourselves in a sea of floating fish. Mitso cut the engine and, together, with the landing-nets we gathered in and shovelled into two large galvanised iron buckets full of seawater, roughly half a hundredweight of fish, not dead, but stunned. Our two large buckets filled – and many more fish filling the bilge of the boat – we made for home.

This, it seemed to me, was not fishing as Father Cyril and I had known it. However, the more immediate problem was what on earth we would do with all this fish. The men and boys on the island could be fed on it for two days. After that, it would be so much rotting garbage. I managed, in my rudimentary Greek, to put the problem to Mitso. '*Tha ta kapnisoume,*' ('We shall smoke them') he said. But where? I wanted to know. '*Tha i thoume,*' ('We'll see') he replied.

Back on the island, everyone was suddenly awake, waiting to take part in our triumphal success. (Alas, poor Erwin was too far gone to join in the celebration.) We sorted out the fish. The red mullet, everyone agreed, should be eaten at once, and Yianni had already revived the big iron stove with wood fuel; its surface was almost, it seemed, red hot. Analysing our catch, we found there were about thirty red mullet of a size matching the Lough Corrib brown trout. These we consumed that night with a simple dressing of oil and lemon, salt and pepper. On Francis, as on me, this feast had an invigorating effect. For the first time, he was thinking of the sea as a source of income which would or could help to bolster the small feudal fief he was establishing on Aghios Nikolaos.

The next morning the sound of hammering announced the construction, by Mitso, of a crude smoking-house, from planks left behind by the builders, and an hour later some twenty large grey mullet were hanging over smoking pine chips and brushwood herbs . . .

But, like all good things, my self-marooning on this loveliest of islands had to come to an end, and in 1936 I found myself running the small popular-music business in the heart of Soho which will

26

be briefly described later in this book. The outbreak of war in 1939 put paid to this business venture, which I had thoroughly enjoyed, and after several infantry training courses I was posted to the Middle East where I was eventually recommended for commissioning. I was encamped in the desert plains near Kirkuk when orders reached me to report to GHQ Cairo.

In Cairo I shared a flat with two other chairborne warriors on the staff at GHQ, and apart from an occasional game of squash at the Gezira Officers' Club, with perhaps a daring visit once a month to Dolls, a nightclub where one could watch, if one felt like it, an ex-mistress of King Farouk doing a belly-dance, our only other interest seemed to be focused on the elegant use of our flywhisks and our comparative expertise in the use of the flit-gun. Any other free time appeared to be taken up with visits to the MO to obtain Sulfa Guanadine, with which we held our recurrent dysentery at bay.

Fish was seldom to be found in Cairo except in restaurants that I could not afford to visit. River fish from the Nile tasted of mud. I was bemused to read recently, in Claudia Roden's *A Book of Middle Eastern Food*, of Cairo street-vendors selling delicious garlicky red mullet. I would have felt I was risking my life by buying fish from a street-vendor.

Having already mentioned the ravishing brunette, Elizabeth Gwynne (later David) at the Ministry of Information in wartime Cairo, it would be churlish of me not to say something further about this enormously talented writer who has brought cookery writing into the mainstream of English literature and stimulated a salutary revolution in British eating habits.

I had been introduced to Elizabeth by Cecil Robson, an exile from his home in Paris and a connoisseur of everything: life and art, food, the theatre (in three languages), fashion and people. I shall always be immensely grateful to him. The meeting with Elizabeth changed my rather jaundiced view of Cairo as a tawdry fly-infested slum. She was generous in sharing her food and her many devoted friends, and I found that, as the range of my culinary and social life expanded, I could face the world without my flywhisk.

How can I try to describe the meals produced for guests by Elizabeth's Sudanese cook, Suleiman, master of the primus stove, when she herself has done it so inimitably in 'Fast and Fresh', one of the pieces in her collected journalism, *An Omelette and a Glass of Wine*? She writes of 'rough but highly flavoured colourful shining vegetable dishes, lentil or fresh tomato soups, delicious spiced pilaffs, lamb kebabs grilled over charcoal, salads with cool mint-flavoured yoghourt dressings, the Egyptian *fellahin* dish of black beans with olive oil and lemon and hard-boiled eggs'. Such dishes did much to reconcile me to the absence of fish.

It was through Elizabeth that I met people like Lawrence Durrell, Robin Fedden and Romney Summers. Her splendid style of dress, often expressed in brilliantly ornate ceremonial kaftans (where on earth did she find them?) made her a unique presence at any function or party she attended, and it can truthfully be added that she attended no function or party which she did not adorn, and enliven with her wit and uninhibited sense of humour.

One particular vignette glitters in my memory – of an evening picnic with Elizabeth, Romney Summers and Robin Fedden, sailing lazily up the Nile. Romney, Elizabeth and I were reclining on cushions, sipping drinks, and Robin was prancing up and down like an elegant monkey in the rigging . . .

Alas, only a few days later I was torn from that happy world, and posted to Istanbul.

The Embassy in Istanbul was only five minutes' walk from Tokatlian's Hotel in Istiklal Caddese which, with its friendly barman and Frenchified Turkish cooking, was a popular rendez-vous for meetings discreet and indiscreet. Those bent on discretion would, in order to avoid the exposure of the public rooms, hire an upper room for an interview to which they would proceed by way of the lift, an ornate affair of glass, mounted in gilt rococo ironwork and of ungenerous size which ensured that any two people travelling in it were thrown into immediate intimacy unless they stood stiffly to attention; they would also, as they rose from floor to floor, come successively under the scrutiny of the hotel servants, spies to a woman and man, hanging about the landings. For me the hotel holds one indelible memory – of the interrupted consumption of one of my favourite dishes, Stuffed Mussels (see page 202) which I was happily consuming with my guest, a Pétainiste operatic soprano of renown and considerable charm. Suddenly there was the appallingly strident sound of an air-raid warning. It cannot have been the only one experienced in Istanbul during the war, but its effect was galvanising. I myself probably started the general panic as I leapt from my chair and, with a brief excuse to my guest, galloped back to the Embassy, where it was my duty to be on such an occasion. People in the street were behaving like the Keystone Kops of Chaplin's early days.

For sheer luxury, I vividly recall having lunch at Abdullah's with the Mrs Consul General of the time, a most generous and outgoing hostess. As a first course I ate caviare wrapped in cylinders of very finely cut smoked salmon, served with a light covering sauce of lemon and cayenne pepper. I dare swear that there was at least a full ounce of the best caviare to each one of the four rolls I consumed.

For lobster dishes, I would repair with friends to an expensive Buyukdere taverna, built over the Bosphorus. Specimens of this marvellous creature would be lifted up from the swift waters below for our inspection and selection, and then served in any way desired. In those days I usually chose lobster salad.

LOBSTER SALAD WITH TARTARE SAUCE

1 large boiled lobster, with coral or roe

for the Tartare Sauce

600ml (1 pint) mayonnaise (see below)

1 dessertspoon each finely chopped chives, capers, parsley, green olives

1 large pickled walnut, crushed

½ teaspoon salt and ½ teaspoon ground black pepper

29

for the salad

---

6 or 7 of the smallest new potatoes, boiled

---

3 hard-boiled eggs, cooked for at least 10 minutes, shelled and quartered

---

2 good bunches *rocca* (rocket) *or* watercress

---

1 bunch purslane

---

the white inner stalks of 1 small head celery, chopped

---

4 tomatoes, peeled and quartered

---

1 large cucumber, cut into slices lengthways, and then cubed

---

3 large red sweet peppers, skinned by grilling (see page 199), seeded, de-pithed and quartered

---

1 dessertspoon mint, finely chopped

---

1 tablespoon parsley, finely chopped

for the salad dressing

---

1 tablespoon onion juice, obtained by salting and sugaring a finely sliced large onion and sieving it over a bowl

---

the flesh of 4 large black olives, crushed

---

2 cloves garlic, crushed and pounded to a purée

---

1 tablespoon lemon juice

---

1 dessertspoon Madeira *or* sweet sherry
1 teaspoon black pepper, crushed

Cut the cooked lobster through from head to tail, dividing it into two parts. At the tail end, search for the narrow black thread–like intestine which you should remove and discard. Set aside in a dish, and reserve any coral or roe, as also all the green and soft parts from just under the head, after the inedible whitish sac has been removed.

Start by making the mayonnaise for the Tartare Sauce.

Mayonnaise
2 egg yolks
1 dessertspoon wine vinegar
¼ teaspoon salt
¼ teaspoon black pepper
600ml (1 pint) pure virgin olive oil

In a bowl, beat the yolks well together with half the vinegar and all the salt and pepper. Now slowly, drop by drop, beat in the olive oil until the mixture begins to thicken. Then gradually increase the flow of oil, beating briskly all the time until the oil is absorbed. Fold in the rest of the vinegar.

To make the Tartare Sauce, incorporate all the other ingredients listed above under this heading into the mayonnaise. Add also, now, the green and soft parts and the coral or roe you have set aside from the lobster.

Extract the tail (this means the body) meat from the lobster, and slice it finely. Line each of the half-shells with 150ml (¼ pint) of the Tartare. Replace the sliced lobster meat in the shells on top of the sauce, and heap the remaining 300ml (½ pint) of sauce over it. Place in a large serving dish and keep in a cool place for half an hour.

Wash, dry thoroughly, and shred by hand the *rocca* (or

watercress) and purslane in the large bowl in which you are going to serve the salad. Arrange the hard-boiled-egg quarters and all the vegetable ingredients on this bed of greenery. Scatter with the mint and parsley. Blend all the salad-dressing ingredients together thoroughly, and pour over the salad. Work the dressing lightly in with your fingers. Set aside in a cool place for half an hour. (Neither the lobster mayonnaise nor the salad should be refrigerated.)

Serves four hungry/greedy people or five/six who are more austere.

Note: It is the privilege of the host to crack the large lobster claws and present them, together with lobster picks, to his two favourite guests. Champagne is the only wine to drink with this admittedly rich and substantial dish. I have memories of a vintage Krug, but I have forgotten the year . . .

I once had the opportunity of visiting Beirut where I was able to sample the intriguing Lebanese fish cuisine (see page 153). Beirut was indeed the 'little Paris of the Middle East', a title to which Limassol in Cyprus – my present home – now, not so convincingly, lays claim. There was some kind of military purpose to my visit but, more importantly, it allowed me to indulge my gourmandise and I even managed to spend a few days at a hill resort.

In Turkey, in the year 1944, time passed swiftly, what with trips in the Embassy's two-masted schooner yacht which took us round the Marmora Islands and across the Marmora Sea to Yalova to bathe in its hot-spring baths. Meanwhile I was doing a crash course in the Russian language, with the strange idea that I might next be posted to Bulgaria to liaise with the Russians. There were no more air-raid warnings, but it was at about this time that the earthquake with which I opened this fishy history occurred, and it was not long before my efforts to wangle a posting to Greece bore fruit.

It was very early in 1945 when I revisited Aghios Nikolaos. I found the house in ruins but as I approached what had been the main entrance I saw that the ancient yellow tile was still in place. I made no bones about taking it with me when I left. Unfortunately this precious reminder of Francis and of my stay on the island had vanished from my jeep when I came to look for it a day later.

2
HEALTH HAPS
AND HAZARDS

I am now nearly eighty and, although I am the grandson, son, nephew and brother of highly qualified doctors, I have absolutely no medical qualifications whatsoever. Such claims as I may make, then, to pontificate, are based only on the close clinical study I have made of one single patient, and that is myself.

You already know that, all my life, I have been dogged – happily enough for me – by fish, my close association with which, in the kitchen and on the table, has enabled me, I claim, to remain young in middle age, and just as young, active, and mentally alive in my seventy-ninth year.

At the age of twenty-one, when I was at Oxford, I applied for membership in the University Air Squadron and on my first trial flight, under preliminary instruction from one Larry Palin in a dual-control DH Moth, we crashed trying to land on Port Meadow, near the Trout Inn at Godstow. I was seriously concussed, suffered damage to my ribcage and had to lie in a dark room for weeks afterwards, but I soon recovered, and there have been no known after-effects. It was probably because of this crash that Colonel Wilkinson, much loved and lamented Dean of Worcester College, better known perhaps, in Territorial Army circles, as 'the Horse', was tempted to prognosticate that if my manner of life did not change I would be dead before I was thirty.

However, at the age of twenty-nine I was undergoing the second of two successive Infantry training courses and one Military Police course. My wartime medical history is a blank except for one violent short bout of sandfly fever in Cyprus.

I was released from the army in 1946: Category A1. Some weeks later I found myself in hospital with double pneumonia, pleurisy and bronchitis, and I was told that, in view of the hopeless state of my lungs, I would be lucky to live for another year. But at the end of that year I found myself volunteering to undergo a serious spinal laminatory operation (since, I believe, discontinued owing to its after-effects on many of my fellow volunteers). Symptoms leading to this operation were incipient paralysis with rapid shrinking of the right leg and acutely painful sciatica.

A long convalescence followed, and I was advised to lead as active and vigorous a life as possible to recover my former physical standards. Fortunately, at that time, I had a good friend who, by pulling a few strings, obtained for me exactly the kind of work that I needed. My first job was involved with the process of collecting silage, which seemed to those concerned almost as important as the harvest itself, and its forking-up and storage in silos. This sometimes became a matter of extreme urgency; the silage collected must not be wet or damp when it goes into storage. In English weather, therefore, the whole operation can become so urgent that speed of gathering it up with a forklift is of the essence. I am proud to say that for several days I managed, without suffocating, to play the punishing rôle of Number One behind the mechanical forklift. Agricultural workers will understand me.

Then there was a relaxed interval of work in the orchards, grafting young apple-tree shoots, wrapping in tissue and boxing perfectly unblemished Cox's Orange Pippins for export and for customers like Fortnum & Mason. Soon again, however, the going became rough. I found myself doing the loneliest and most frightening job there is.

34

The distributor, as he may be thought of, stands in this enormous silo, fifty foot high, into which, through a huge canvas tube, powerful pumps pour all the dust and debris of the harvest, sometimes enriched with industrial molasses. For the solitary distributor within, there seems to be no means of communicating with the outside world as he stumbles around, spreading the silage and stamping it down. God help him if he cannot keep pace with the inflow of the demon pump. There he stands, fighting for his life, and no one even to see or hear him as he drowns in straw dust. The sentinel of Pompeii immediately comes to mind, as he waits for the lava from Vesuvius to overwhelm him.

I survived, and am eternally grateful to those who gave me the opportunity to rise to these physical challenges. Then I became a thatcher's mate. This particular thatcher, though following the Norfolk reed methods, used a Devon wheatstraw reed instead, and as his mate my duty was first, with a sickle reaper, to slice off from the thicker end of the stook a half-inch of its length – no easy task itself; then to climb the ladder to hand the stook to the thatcher; then to run like mad into the interior, climb up to the battened roof, and accept the enormous needle which, threaded with thick Norwegian tarred twine, would be thrust through for me to bind tightly round a batten; and then to thrust the needle back at the thatcher for the process to be repeated hundreds of times before the day's work was done.

This was undoubtedly the hardest work I have ever been called upon to perform in my life; when I had done my stint my convalescence could be considered over, and I was again a whole man.

Some years later, when I was in business as a trader in the antiques market in London, I was found to be suffering from a lung abscess and was sent to an excellent hospital, specialising in lung diseases, outside Maidstone. It was the policy of the hospital to operate quickly, whenever possible, in such cases. On this occasion, however, I refused to cooperate, and was treated instead with large daily doses of Terramycin for six weeks. The abscess vanished, and after a few weeks' convalescence I took up work again. That was twenty-five years ago, and I have had no recurrence of this trouble.

In the medical episodes described above, I have been treated by skilled doctors and surgeons and also by chemotherapy. I would like to claim, though, that my continuing devotion to fish –

which, at all relevant convalescent times, was a major part of my diet – played a dominant part in my speedy recuperation to full and active good health.

In 1974, I got married for the fourth time. We were both keen party-goers and delighted in dancing to jazz and swing music in a casual solo style. At one party I remember dancing – or preening and showing off – in this quiet rhythmic way for most of the night, without the slightest subsequent sensation of exhaustion. This way of dancing, first practised by me in my college rooms at Oxford, is the finest tonic exercise for the human body.

Throughout this period, when I was in my middle sixties, I felt as fit as a fiddle, and in the opinion of my wife and all our friends I appeared to be no more than forty-five years old. This inhibition of the normally much swifter onset of old age I definitely attribute to the regular intake of fresh fish. Grilled herrings, crabs, mussels, scallops, prawns, skate, monkfish – these were among my favourites, my staples on the Bermondsey and Portobello markets being freshly boiled crabs and prawns: so easy to break open and consume on a market stall.

All was going swimmingly in Highbury Fields, Islington, where we lived. The happy atmosphere obtaining there is best reflected by verses from a poem by Thomas Jordan (1612–85):

> Let us drink and be merry, dance, joke and rejoice,
> With claret and sherry, theorbo and voice!
> The changeable world to our joy is unjust.
>> All treasure's uncertain,
>> Then down with your dust!
> In frolics disperse your pounds, shillings and pence,
> For we shall be nothing a hundred years hence.
>
> We'll sport and be free with Moll, Betty and Dolly,
> Have oysters and lobsters to cure melancholy;
>> Fish dinners will make a man spring like a flea.
>> Dame Venus, love's lady,
>> Was born of the sea;
> With her and with Bacchus we'll tickle the sense,
> For we shall be past it a hundred years hence.

The pastoral and lyric domestic scene suggested above suddenly came to an end when, without any previous warning, I was attacked by the disabling and painful symptoms of arthritis. As it was thought that the rigours of the London climate and the nature of my work, in the early hours, often before dawn, on the market, might be to some extent responsible for my complaint, we decided, when a lucky opportunity offered – the success of our first published books – to migrate to Cyprus where sun and sea-bathing might bring relief if not an outright cure. However, as time passed, there was little or no improvement, and although I could manage to help with the cooking and such entertainment as we could afford, and although I could dance around on the veranda to traditional jazz, I couldn't feel happy, unable to lift my right arm high enough to shave myself or to control a pen well enough to sign a recognisable version of my own signature on a cheque.

As I have suggested, before coming to Cyprus, my wife and I, both fish-lovers, always considered fish the most important part of our diet. In Cyprus where fish taverns abound and a wide variety of fish – though mostly small in size – is available, we greatly increased our intake of fish. Apart from my disabling arthritis we both felt fighting fit, and there was a general feeling of euphoria about the house.

What I am about to reveal may be taken as some kind of claim that I experienced a miraculous cure of my arthritis, and that the event was directly due to our almost exclusively fish diet. Not so! I make no claim of that sort. The facts are as follows.

One afternoon I was playing on the veranda with our beautiful cat, Retsina. I was trying to throw a ping-pong ball at her, but was quite unable to accomplish the simple movement required. The very next morning I went on to the veranda and, with my hitherto 'lame' hand, gripped a tennis-ball lying on top of the old peasant cupboard that stands there; remembering the style of Frank Woolley, a famous bowler of my youth, of whom more later, I lifted my arm up, up, as high as it would go over my shoulder to deliver a splendid 'yorker' at the enormous *monstera deliciosa* plant which grows against the end wall. There was absolutely no pain and, to confirm this wonder, I swung my arm around over and over again. Not a trace of pain! My arthritis had simply vanished.

I am told that these sudden remissions of disabling conditions often occur, but this happened some five years ago, and there has been no sign of a return of any of my previous symptoms.

3
THE LASSALLE
FISH REGIMEN

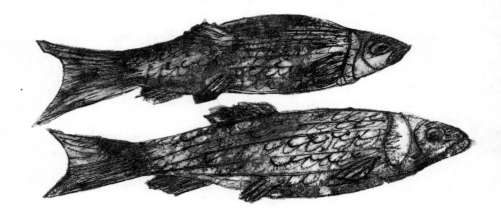

My general disapproval of deep-fat frying in batter was temporarily withdrawn when, living in Islington, my wife and I would frequent the Albion public house where this form of cookery was carried out to perfection by Flo Heath, the comely and lovable wife of Bill, the landlord. The quality of plaice and flounder used, and Flo's magic touch with the batter, almost converted me to this way of cooking fish.

The supplier of this very high-quality fish was Steve Hatt, a neighbourhood fishmonger in Essex Road.★ One of Steve Hatt's working stocklists is shown opposite. Such fish as do not appear on this list, which is liable to change several times a day, can always be quickly obtained on request. Hatt's Sevruga and Beluga Russian caviare and his shellfish from all over the world are reputedly the finest that can be supplied anywhere in London. Long may he live to practise his skilled craft.

★Steve Hatt, 88 Essex Road, Islington, London N1 (tel. 01–226 3963).

Steve Hatt's Fish List

Plaice

Plaice Fil.

Lemon S.

Dover S. Large

Dover S. Small

Turbot

Salmon

Salmon Trout

Rainbow Trout

Had. Fil.

Cod Fil.

Jumbo

Cod

Skate

Oysters

Monk

Makerel

Coley

Herrings

Halibut

Soft Roe

Grey Mullet

Red Mullet

Whiting

Squid

Sprats

Sm. Had

Sm. Cut

Sardines

Sm. Had. F.

Bloaters

Kippers

Prawns

King Prawns

Peeled Prawns

Scampi

Scallops

Time was, some eight years ago, when many of us believed that the English fishmonger was a dying species. That Steve Hatt survives and greatly flourishes is only one sign of what could be called a renaissance in the country's fishing industry. The credit for this revival must go to the Ministry of Agriculture, Fisheries & Food and to the Sea Fish Industry Authority who have together, in the last few years, spent some eight million pounds not only in direct investment but in effective promotional and informational campaigns on a lavish scale.

There now follows an induction into the recipes for the Lassalle diet. All these recipes have the same routine structure. They begin with the construction of a miniature *court-bouillon;* in effect an aromatic vegetable and herb stock with spices added. The amount of herbs, vegetables and spices specified may appear excessive, but this lavish provision is intentional, my purpose being that from the moment you venture into using these recipes, your kitchen will become redolent of the evergreen thickets of the maquis in Southern France which were half the lure of such places as Cap d'Antibes in its days of innocence. The herbs, vegetables and spices I prescribe are nowadays easy to obtain in England. As to oven temperatures and cooking times I must admit that there is, superficially, a bit of a problem. Here in Cyprus I cook from gas supplied from a cylinder placed near the stove, and the pressure varies a good deal with climatic conditions and with the amount of gas left in the cylinder. Throughout the recipes I have prescribed Gas 7/220°C/425°F, as I have found that, at this temperature and on the times given, my oven produces splendidly cooked, but not over-cooked fish. I am sure that your own oven, which no doubt works perfectly, will enable you to arrive at accurate timings very soon.

The diet element of the regimen

1 This diet is not a slimming diet, but can easily be converted into one by cutting down sharply on the high-calorie foods: ie, potatoes, pulses, rice, bread and pasta.

2 Cut all meat from your daily intake. Reduce to the minimum your intake of butter and other saturated fats and high-cholesterol foods. Limit yourself to two eggs a week. Avoid

food containing refined sugar, which can do you nothing but harm.

3 Eat plenty of vegetables in season, salads and fresh fruit. You may also eat pulses (beans, lentils), rice, wholemeal bread, crispbread and wholemeal pasta.

4 The central positive element of the diet is the willing pledge, on the part of those who wish to follow it, to consume at least 225g (8oz) of fish a day, cooked in the manner given on page 43. This method of cooking has been selected as that which best ensures the retention of all the health-giving elements, essential fats, enzymes and vitamins of the fish; in addition, as the fish cooks with the herbs and spices specified, it produces from its own juices an idiosyncratic and delicious sauce. This *en papillote* method has now, for many cooks, superseded poaching and braising. The essential feature in these recipes is the miniature *court-bouillon* which I am convinced lies at the very heart of European cuisine.

5 Followers of the diet should pledge themselves to persevere for at least the initial course of thirty days, for which I have supplied recipes. At the end of that time I can safely promise you that you will be conscious of a resurgence of your life force in all its aspects, not least in a general sense of euphoria and a notable increase in your mental energy.

What your government thinks about fish

Fish is nutritionally as near-perfect a food as you are likely to find. It is extremely low in carbohydrates and saturated fat, yet bursting with high-quality proteins – all the ones you need for good health. All types of fish are a good source of B vitamins and minerals such as iodine needed for the body's metabolism and calcium needed for growth.

Oily fish, such as mackerel, sardines and tunny fish – so-called because the oil is distributed throughout the flesh rather than being concentrated in the liver as it is in white fish – are particularly rich in vitamins. Vitamin D helps build bones while vitamin A, found in very few foods, is a real beautifier. It encourages good sight and keeps the skin healthy and moist.

Oily fish are also high in polyunsaturated fats – those not associated with heart disease and high cholesterol levels – and the best source of the fat the body needs for all-round health.

Research now suggests that a couple of fish meals a week may actually lower the cholesterol level in the blood.

The nutritional value of fish

*Analysis per ounce based on raw edible portions of flesh

	Cod or Haddock	Herring	Beef	Lamb	Pork	Chicken
Protein (g)	4.9	4.8	4.9	4.5	4.5	5.0
Fat (g)	0.2	5.2	6.9	8.6	8.2	5.0
Calories (kcal)	21	66	75	95	92	65
Calcium (mg)	5	9	2	2	2	3
Iron (mg)	0.1	0.2	0.5	0.4	0.2	0.2
Vitamin A (mg)	0	13	0	0	0	0
Vitamin D (mg)	0	6.4	0	0	0	0
Thiamine (mg)	0.02	0	0.01	0.02	0.17	0.02
Riboflavin (mg)	0.02	0.05	0.05	0.05	0.05	0.04
Nicotinic acid (mg)	1.4	2	2.1	2.1	2	2.6

*Ministry of Agriculture, Fisheries & Food Manual of Nutrition

In the *Sunday Telegraph* of June 1988 I was delighted to come upon the following item:

> Professor Michael Crawford, a biochemist at the Institute of Zoology in London's Regent's Park, has an extraordinary explanation for why Britain ruled the waves, until the rise of the food-processing industry. He points out that a staple in the diet of the crafty Cockneys, who lived around the Thames Estuary, was seafood which is exceptionally rich in essential fats, so-called because they are vital to health and life itself, and which make up most of the solid part of our brain and central nervous system ... Professor Crawford believes that Bertie Wooster, who ascribed the great brain of his man Jeeves to his great love of fish, may well have been right.

With the above facts before you, is it not a duty to try the effects of a month on the fish regimen?

Cooking the fish for the Lassalle regimen

The structure and method of cooking for the recipes which follow have been reduced, through practical trial and testing, to the simplest of routine procedures. Each requires only three stages of cooking after the assembly of the ingredients for the miniature *court-bouillon:* spices, herbs and aromatic vegetables suited to the particular fish to be cooked.

1 Bring all the ingredients to the boil together in the 150ml (¼ pint) of water specified in each recipe (except for Brill Italienne [page 61] and Sea-bream with Red Wine [page 67]), and simmer for 15 minutes.

2 Pass this mixture through a blender or food processor to make a loose purée or, in some cases, a thickened liquid.

3 Make the fish selected into two parcels (as shown in the diagram below), with the puréed mixture and the 25g (1oz) of butter

(specified in the recipes) being divided between them. If desired, the butter in each parcel can be replaced by a dessertspoon of olive oil or, if you prefer it, by one of the many flavourless vegetable oils available. The 'sealed' airtight parcel is then put into a preheated oven on a baking tin or dish (also preheated), and cooked at Gas 7/220°C/425°F (see page 40) for the time prescribed in the recipe.

In the diagram I have shown the fish served in its packet and opened at the table, so that its delicious fragrance fills the air. If you do not want to do this, you can remove the fish, in its miniature sauce, to a dish in the kitchen. But the first way is far better, and is the one prescribed in all 'classic' recipes.

Notes: a All the recipes given here are for two people. It is a simple matter of adjusting quantities if you want to cook for more, or just for yourself.

b Fresh herbs are always best, but if you can't obtain the ones specified, it is possible to use dried ones. These are much stronger and you should use one-third of the given quantity.

DOVER SOLE
WITH MUSSELS

Cooking time: 12 minutes

This is a blending together of two of the finest seafood flavours. The Dover sole has deservedly held its position as one of the choicest of seafoods, both in flavour and texture, since fine cooking began. Here, allied to mussels, whose juices mingle with its own as it cooks in its parcel, it is hard to beat.

450g (1lb) skinned fillets Dover sole

1 pint mussels, unopened

25g (1oz) butter

for the court-bouillon

150ml (¼ pint) water

2 tablespoons dry white wine

the white of 1 small leek, chopped

1 shallot, chopped

1 small green pepper,
seeded and chopped

3 sprigs parsley

1 dessertspoon thyme

1 bay leaf
(to be removed before blending)

½ teaspoon salt

This is a splendid dish to launch our recipes with, and I believe you will return to it again and again. You could use other high-quality non-oily fish, such as turbot, brill or John Dory.

TURBOT WITH FENNEL ROOT AND SWEET PEPPERS

Cooking time: 12–15 minutes

This fish probably ranks only second to sole in white-fish aristocracy; its skin is delicious.

for the parcels

450g (1lb) turbot fillets *or* small steaks, unskinned

25g (1oz) butter

for the court-bouillon

150ml (¼ pint) water

3 tablespoons dry white wine

1 tablespoon fennel root, chopped

2 sweet green peppers, seeded and chopped

3 spring onions, chopped

2 black peppercorns, crushed

2 good pinches salt

SALMON WITH DILL
AND CAPERS

Cooking time: 16 minutes

Salmon and dill make natural companions in the kitchen, hence the emphasis given to dill in this recipe.

for the parcels

450g (1lb) salmon fillets *or* thin steaks

25g (1oz) butter

for the court-bouillon

150ml (¼ pint) water

2 tablespoons dry white wine

1 dessertspoon Italian vermouth

1 small cucumber, peeled and chopped

2 small gherkins, chopped

2 tablespoons capers, chopped

3 tablespoons chopped dill

HUSS, DOGFISH
OR PORBEAGLE
WITH CELERIAC

Cooking time: 16–20 minutes

These splendid fish of the small shark family are in the lower price-range, and are well worth getting to know.

for the parcels

450g (1lb) fillets huss, dogfish or
porbeagle, skinned

25g (1oz) butter

for the court-bouillon

150ml (¼ pint) water

1 tablespoon dry white wine

1 teaspoon white wine vinegar

1 tablespoon chopped celeriac

1 medium-sized onion, chopped

1 small green pepper,
seeded and chopped

1 thin slice of a garlic clove

2 anchovy fillets, chopped

2 sprigs parsley

1 teaspoon thyme

3 black peppercorns, crushed

NEAPOLITAN
MONKFISH

Cooking time: 16 minutes

The monkfish has a distinct flavour of shellfish, and when cooked
with scallops, as here, this flavour is strongly brought out.

for the parcels

450g (1lb) fillets of monkfish tail,
skinned

4 small shelled scallops
(their skirts removed) chopped together
with their coral or roe

25g (1oz) butter

for the court-bouillon

150ml (¼ pint) water

2 tablespoons dry red wine

1 tablespoon tomato purée

1 teaspoon made English mustard

1 dessertspoon horseradish cream

½ teaspoon best quality soya sauce

1 dessertspoon parsley, chopped

1 dessertspoon thyme, chopped

1 tablespoon chopped basil

½ teaspoon ground cumin

SCALLOPS WITH MUSSELS

Cooking time: 15 minutes

Here two exquisite flavours are combined and enhanced. In this recipe, the cooked and blended ingredients are bland and do not smother the flavours of the shellfish.

for the parcels

450g (1lb) shelled scallops
(their skirts removed), chopped together
with their coral or roe

300g (12oz) unopened mussels

25g (1oz) butter

for the court-bouillon

150ml (¼ pint) water

2 tablespoons dry white wine

1 spring onion, chopped

1 dessertspoon chopped parsley

1 teaspoon chopped thyme

2 crushed black peppercorns

a pinch of salt

Your parcels will have to be rather larger than usual, containing, as each does, 150g (6oz) of unopened mussels. (Any mussels still unopened after cooking should, of course, be discarded.)

TROUT WITH OLIVES

Cooking time: 12 minutes

For this recipe, the *court-bouillon* ingredients are left uncooked.
You proceed straight to blending.

for the parcels

2 × 225g (8oz) trout, cleaned but not
skinned, and with heads and tails removed

2 bay leaves (one on each trout)

25g (1oz) butter

for the (uncooked) court-bouillon

150ml (¼ pint) water

2 tablespoons dry white wine

1 tablespoon chopped chives

3 large black olives, stoned and chopped

PLAICE WITH ARTICHOKES

Cooking time: 12 minutes

Plaice is a very greatly underestimated fish!

for the parcels

450g (1lb) fillets plaice,
with the black skin left on

25g (1oz) butter

for the court-bouillon

150ml (¼ pint) water

2 tablespoons dry white wine

the white of 2 small leeks, chopped

2 small artichoke hearts, chopped

2 spring onions, chopped

1 small carrot, chopped

1 anchovy fillet, chopped

1 tablespoon chopped parsley

4 black peppercorns, crushed

1 bay leaf
(to be removed before blending)

1 clove
(to be removed before blending)

Fillets of large whiting (skinned) or of lemon sole (the black skin left on) can also be used for this recipe.

HALIBUT WITH
CAPERS AND OLIVES

Cooking time: 18–20 minutes

Halibut is a worthy and reliable fish. It is the largest flat fish found in the sea, reaches enormous weights, and lives to a venerable old age.

for the parcels

450g (1lb) fillets halibut, skinned

25g (1oz) butter

for the court-bouillon

150ml (¼ pint) water

2 tablespoons dry red wine

juice of ½ lemon

1 dessertspoon tomato purée

1 stick celery, chopped

3 large black olives, stoned and chopped

1 tablespoon chopped capers

4 black peppercorns, crushed

COD WITH LEEKS
AND HERBS

Cooking time: 16 minutes

One French master-chef considers cod to be the finest fish of all. Its unique flavour, when fresh, regrettably fades when it is frozen.

for the parcels

450g (1lb) cod fillets *or* steaks, skinned

25g (1oz) butter

for the court-bouillon

150ml (¼ pint) water

2 tablespoons dry white wine

the white of 3 small leeks, chopped

1 tablespoon chopped parsley

1 teaspoon ground allspice

3 black peppercorns, crushed

2 good pinches salt

Fillets of (skinned) fresh haddock can also be used for this recipe.

FRESH HADDOCK
WITH MUSHROOMS

Cooking time: 16 minutes

---

for the parcels

450g (1lb) fresh haddock fillets, skinned

25g (1oz) butter

---

for the court-bouillon

150ml (¼ pint) water

---

2 tablespoons dry white wine

---

juice of ½ lemon

100g (4oz) fresh mushrooms, chopped

---

1 teaspoon chopped chives

½ teaspoon grated nutmeg

---

4 black peppercorns, crushed

---

2 good pinches salt

Fillets of cod can also be used for this recipe.

SKATE WITH CELERIAC

Cooking time: 18 minutes

Wings of skate are usually served poached and dressed with black butter. However, they are very good cooked in other ways, as here.

for the parcels

2 × 225g (8oz) wings of skate

25g (1oz) butter

for the court-bouillon

150ml (¼ pint) water

1 tablespoon dry white wine

1 dessertspoon white wine vinegar

2 tablespoons celeriac, chopped

2 small green peppers,
seeded and chopped

1 anchovy fillet, chopped

1 clove garlic, skinned and crushed

4 black peppercorns, crushed

1 good sprig rosemary
(to be removed before blending)

2 bay leaves
(to be removed before blending)

Skinned fillets of huss, dogfish or porbeagle can also be used for this recipe.

COLEY WITH
SWEET PEPPERS

Cooking time: 12 minutes

Coley has rather a yellowish-grey colour on the fishmonger's slab, but this disappears when it is cooked. It is in the lower price-range and is looked down on by many, but not by me.

for the parcels

450g (1lb) fillets coley, skinned

25g (1oz) butter

for the court-bouillon

150ml (¼ pint) water

1 tablespoon dry white wine

3 sweet red peppers, seeded and chopped

1 shallot, chopped

1 dessertspoon parsley, chopped

3 black peppercorns, crushed

2 good pinches salt

SWORDFISH WITH ROSEMARY

Swordfish is commonly grilled, but it is also very good cooked in parcels, as here.

for the parcels

2 × 225g (8oz) swordfish steaks

25g (1oz) butter *or*
(particularly good in this recipe)
1 tablespoon olive oil

for the court-bouillon

150ml (¼ pint) water

2 tablespoons dry white wine

2 good sprigs rosemary (these should be
removed from the mixture before
blending, and one placed on each
swordfish steak)

3 black peppercorns, crushed

1 scant teaspoon ground ginger

½ clove garlic, crushed

2 good pinches salt

FRESH TUNNY
WITH SPICES

Cooking time: 18 minutes

The tunny (tuna) can sometimes be dry, and is improved by a very
loose purée, as here.

for the parcels
2 × 225g (8oz) tunny steaks
25g (1oz) butter (this is another recipe in which 1 tablespoon olive oil would be even nicer)

for the court-bouillon
150ml (¼ pint) water
2 tablespoons dry white wine
1 dessertspoon white wine vinegar
juice of ½ lemon
1 dessertspoon made English mustard
1 dessertspoon horseradish cream
2 shallots, chopped
1 teaspoon ground allspice

SCALLOPS, PRAWNS
AND MUSSELS,
TÊTE-À-TÊTE

Cooking time: 15 minutes

A glorious union, here, of my favourite seafoods . . .

for the parcels

450g (1lb) small shelled scallops
(their skirts removed) chopped together
with their coral or roe

a few prawns, boiled, shelled
and cut into strips vertically

12 mussels, unopened

25g (1oz) butter

for the court-bouillon

150ml (¼ pint) water

2 tablespoons medium-dry white wine

1 dessertspoon each chopped parsley,
thyme and chives

2 drops Tabasco sauce

a pinch of salt

BRILL ITALIENNE

Cooking time: 12–15 minutes

Brill and chicken turbot rank, in my opinion, with Dover sole, as the finest-tasting of the flat fish; grown turbot come next, with halibut very much an also-ran.

for the parcels
450g (1lb) brill fillets *or* steaks, skinned
25g (1oz) butter

for the court-bouillon
150ml (¼ pint) fresh tomato juice
2 tablespoons dry white wine
1 green and 1 red sweet pepper, seeded and chopped
2 small anchovy fillets, chopped
1 dessertspoon each of parsley and basil, chopped
1 clove of garlic, crushed

Fillets of Dover sole, John Dory or turbot can also be used for this recipe.

SPRING-TIME
SALMON TROUT

Cooking time: 15 minutes

Salmon trout (also known as sea-trout) is, to me, as delicious in taste as salmon, and also more finely textured.

for the parcels

2 × 225g (8oz) salmon trout, scaled, cleaned, and with heads and tails removed

25g (1oz) butter

for the court-bouillon

150ml (¼ pint) water

2 tablespoons dry white wine

juice of ½ lemon

1 tablespoon onion, chopped

1 small carrot, grated

1 tablespoon chopped celery heart

2 small gherkins, chopped

1 dessertspoon chopped dill

1 tablespoon chopped parsley

3 black peppercorns, crushed

2 good pinches salt

Salmon steaks (5cm/2in) can also be cooked by this method.

HERRINGS IN A
SHARP SAUCE

Cooking time: 12 minutes

Here is man's greatest nutritional life-support system, beautifully packaged in a single fish. (If you like, you can eat a herring a day and forget all the other recipes given here.... but it might get a bit monotonous.)

for the parcels

2 × 225g (8oz) herrings, cleaned, scaled,
and with heads and tails removed

25g (1oz) butter

for the court-bouillon

150ml (¼ pint) water

1 tablespoon dry white wine

1 dessertspoon made English mustard

1 dessertspoon onion, chopped

1 dessertspoon chopped capers

2 small gherkins, chopped

1 teaspoon dill, chopped

Mackerel can also be used for this recipe, which is very similar to the one that follows.

MACKEREL IN A SHARP SAUCE

Cooking time: 12 minutes

for the parcels

2 × 225g (8oz) mackerel, cleaned,
scaled, and with heads and tails removed

25g (1oz) butter

for the court-bouillon

150ml (¼ pint) water

2 tablespoons dry white wine

1 teaspoon wine vinegar

1 dessertspoon made English mustard

1 small anchovy fillet, chopped

1 dessertspoon chopped onion

1 dessertspoon chopped capers

1 dessertspoon dill, chopped

Herrings can also be used for this recipe.

SEA-BASS WITH FENNEL

Cooking time: 15 minutes

Small bass lack the flavour of the large ones, and there are problems with the small bones. There are no problems, however, with steaks from a large bass, as specified here.

for the parcels

2 × 225g (8oz) steaks from a large bass

25g (1oz) butter

for the court-bouillon

150ml (¼ pint) water

2 tablespoons dry white wine

juice of ½ lemon

2 tablespoons chopped fennel root

1 tablespoon chopped onion

1 tablespoon chopped celery

1 small carrot, grated

1 small gherkin, chopped

1 dessertspoon chopped dill

1 tablespoon chopped parsley

3 black peppercorns, crushed

a good pinch of salt

GURNARD WITH MUSSELS

Cooking time: 15 minutes

The gurnard, with its large 'bulldozer' head, is a firm, white-fleshed fish of fine taste. With its head and tail removed, it is much reduced in weight, which is why I have recommended larger fish for this recipe.

for the parcels

2 × 300g (11oz) gurnards, cleaned, scaled, and with heads and tails removed

10 mussels, unopened

25g (1oz) butter

for the court-bouillon

150ml (¼ pint) water

1 tablespoon dry white wine

juice of ½ lemon

1 dessertspoon *tahina*

2 shallots, finely chopped

1 tablespoon each parsley and thyme, chopped

1 pinch cumin

4 black peppercorns, ground

a pinch of salt

SEA-BREAM WITH RED WINE

Cooking time: 12–15 minutes

As with sea-bass (page 65) steaks from large fish are better than whole small ones because of the bones; the flavour is better, too.

for the parcels

2 × 225g (8oz) steaks from a large sea-bream

25g (1oz) butter

for the court-bouillon

150ml (¼ pint) good dry red wine

1 tablespoon tomato purée

1 teaspoon best soya sauce

1 tablespoon fennel root, chopped

1 clove garlic, crushed

1 tablespoon each finely chopped parsley and thyme

3 black peppercorns, crushed

GARFISH WITH MUSSELS

Cooking time: 15 minutes

This is the splendid fish with the long 'beak' and, when cooked, the green bones. Shorn of its head and tail, it is here cut *across* the body into two equal portions. (It is nice to keep the bone, because of its startling colour.)

for the parcels

2 × 225g (8oz) portions obtained from 1 × 675g (1½lb) garfish, cleaned, scaled, and with head and tail removed, then cut across the body

8 mussels, unopened

25g (1oz) butter

for the court-bouillon

150ml (¼ pint) water

2 tablespoons dry white wine

1 shallot, chopped

1 sweet pepper (red or green), seeded and chopped

1 tablespoon chopped parsley

½ teaspoon ground allspice

2 drops Tabasco sauce

2 good pinches salt

GREY MULLET WITH ROSEMARY

Cooking time: 12 minutes

This is a rather negative fish, with no specially defined taste of its own. It is, however, quick to cook, and much improved by rosemary.

for the parcels

2 × 225g (8oz) grey mullet, cleaned, scaled, and with head and tail removed

25g (1oz) butter

for the court-bouillon

150ml (¼ pint) water

2 tablespoons dry white wine

1 medium-sized onion, chopped

1 tablespoon chopped celery

1 tablespoon chopped parsley

2 sprigs rosemary (to be removed before blending and placed on the fish)

1 teaspoon ground allspice

3 black peppercorns, crushed

2 pinches salt

SMALL PIKE IN A SHARP SAUCE

Cooking time: 15 minutes

I gather that very large pike appear more frequently in British fishmonger's shops than they do here in Cyprus, where small ones are the rule. Steaks from a larger pike can be used instead of halved small pike, making allowances for cooking time which, in the case of steaks, should be increased to 35 minutes.

for the parcels

1 small pike, weighing about 675g (1½lb), cleaned, scaled, and with head and tail removed; then cut across the body into two portions, each weighing roughly 225g (8oz)

25g (1oz) butter

for the court-bouillon

150ml (¼ pint) water

2 tablespoons dry white wine

1 teaspoon white wine vinegar

1 dessertspoon horseradish cream

2 shallots, chopped

2 tablespoons parsley, chopped

1 teaspoon ground allspice

3 drops Tabasco sauce

70

SNAPPER, STRONGLY SEASONED

Cooking time: 15 minutes

These reddish fish are now in many British fishmonger's shops. Though very inexpensive, they are good eating, but need an emphatic sauce.

for the parcels

2 × 225g (8oz) snappers, cleaned, scaled, and with heads and tails removed

25g (1oz) butter

for the court-bouillon

150ml (¼ pint) water

2 tablespoons dry white wine

1 tablespoon tomato purée

1 teaspoon best soya sauce

2 green sweet peppers, seeded and chopped

1 clove garlic, crushed

1 teaspoon ground coriander seed

1 teaspoon ground allspice

1 teaspoon ground ginger

2 drops Tabasco sauce

PORBEAGLE WITH SPICES

Cooking time: 16–20 minutes

for the parcels

450g (1lb) fillets porbeagle

25g (1oz) butter

for the court-bouillon

150ml (¼ pint) water

2 tablespoons dry white wine

juice of ½ lemon

2 shallots, chopped

2 small anchovy fillets, chopped

4 black peppercorns, crushed

1 dessertspoon each parsley and thyme, chopped

1 scant teaspoon cumin

This recipe is also suitable for fillets of huss and dogfish and for wings of skate.

MEDITERRANEAN MONKFISH

Cooking time: 16 minutes

for the parcels

450g (1lb) fillets monkfish

25g (1oz) butter

for the court-bouillon

150ml (¼ pint) water

2 tablespoons Marsala (or Madeira)

1 dessertspoon lemon juice

1 tablespoon tomato purée

2 black olives, stoned and chopped

2 anchovy fillets, chopped

3 cloves garlic, crushed

1 tablespoon basil, chopped

HOT CONGER

Cooking time: 25 minutes

A firm, juicy fish whose strong flavour can stand up to a strong and peppery sauce.

for the parcels

450g (1lb) steaks of a young skinned
conger (avoid the bony tail-end)

25g (1oz) butter

for the court-bouillon

150ml (¼ pint) water

juice of ½ lemon

2 tablespoons tomato purée

3 small dried red chillies,
minced with their seeds,
or 2 teaspoons hot red chilli sauce

3 cloves garlic, crushed

1 tablespoon parsley, finely chopped

1 heaped teaspoon cumin

2 good pinches salt

Any members of the small shark family such as huss, dogfish, porbeagle, can be cooked according to this recipe, but for only 16–20 minutes.

Postscript: I have given thirty recipes, but you can, of course, substitute one for another, as you choose. (If you like, you can use recipes for cheaper fish and avoid the very expensive ones.) I should also like you to make your own variations on the *court-bouillons,* as the fancy takes you.

4
KINETIC ASPECTS OF THE LASSALLE REGIMEN

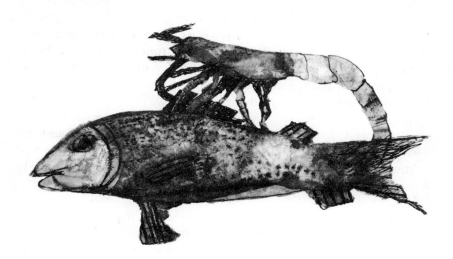

Creative Nostalgia

Behind my regime lies the belief that, to keep going and to prevent the onset of premature senility, it is not enough merely to exercise the body. The body and mind should be continually in motion, rhythmically and imaginatively, together.

Nostalgia is common to us all – and not necessarily a good thing. Simply to sit, constantly regretting the past, repeating to oneself, *'Mais où sont les neiges d'antan?'* ('Where are the snows of yesteryear?') is not purposeful. To ward off the onset of senility, nostalgia must become – by the conscious, deliberate exercise of the imagination – creative, and impel the body and mind to continuous movement. Once nostalgia becomes creative, it acquires tremendous power.

How to show this? . . . I can at least hint at it by giving an example of its most powerful expression in song. It comes from Psalm 137: By the waters of Babylon we sat down and wept: when we remembered thee, O Sion. The collective creative nostalgia of a whole race of enslaved exiles is shown in this psalm. Originating from the same source is the creative nostalgia of Black American gospel song. Any early recording of Mahalia Jackson, belting out the eternal lament, will convey the feeling of power which haunts early jazz. These two examples may help to convey the meaning of my term, 'creative nostalgia'. To put it in a more personal context: through imaginative mime, creative nostalgia harnesses past experiences and emotions, to free us from the enslavement of the ageing process.

Throughout the ages, mime itself has always been considered as a simple form of magic. It was believed that if you mimed a man you admired, you could in some sense become him, and his virtues and powers would flow into you. This was beneficent or 'white' magic. If you hated someone, you mimed him by making a wax image of him, stuck pins in it and shut it away in a drawer – 'black' magic.

I myself use only 'white' magic. I use it for purposes of health. I no longer play football and other games, nor do I 'jog'. I get physical – and mental – exercise by creative mime of various nostalgic activities.

Jazz

Having conquered America, jazz leapt across the Atlantic Ocean in the middle of the 1920s, sweeping Beethoven aside on the way, to arrive triumphantly in the cultural centres of Europe, notably England, rapidly establishing a strong jazz cult.

By the time I arrived at Oxford, in 1929, the cult had already taken firm root in many of the colleges, 'Wuggins' among them, and my own rooms soon became a sort of shrine to such heady performers as Miff Mole and his Washboard Beaters. We were, of course, very ignorant and unselective, seeking only the excitement of new rhythms and the undoubted pleasures of showing off the elegance of our figures as we solo-danced, peacocking around the room to the throb and beat of this new hypnotic music.

I would say that the centre of the 'trad' movement, in my day, was a Trinity lodging-house called the Old Parsonage, now a hotel, at the northernmost end of St Giles. The incumbent of these exquisite medieval lodgings was Francis Astley; 'Bones' to his friends, who were many. 'Bones' was a Classics scholar and a hockey blue. At weekends the Old Parsonage became a Soho jazz jam session – on records, of course – and it was here that the art of peacocking around, and showing off in a voluptuous manner, was perfected.

(On a more serious note, the Old Parsonage represented, at the time, a bastion against, and a retreat from, the impertinent intrusions into our personal affairs of the members of the falsely named 'Oxford Group', then rapidly gaining ground in the university. All jazzmen, by definition, loathed the very idea of Buchmanism, with its sickly parody of the confessional service, filched from old Quaker ideas, and perverted.)

Although the Old Parsonage, and all it meant to me, forms part of that nostalgic memory which I can vividly recall, there is one aborted jazz party at which little dancing was done which, in imagination, I can bring back, as a stimulus to jazz mime, in Technicolor brilliance, in every detail.

The incident was critical to my whole future and led to my being rusticated from college. The date was Friday 13 January, which should have put me on my guard. It was a week exactly before my twenty-first birthday. Returning from a shave and haircut, I went into my rooms to find a comparative stranger ensconced in my only armchair, by the fire. I glanced up at my bookshelves. No, both *Ulysses* and *Les Oeuvres Badines de Piron* were there still.

'Hello,' I said.

'Oh, hello. Sorry to intrude. Your oak wasn't sported.'

'It seldom is,' I replied.

'To explain,' he went on, 'a fellow in your college seems to think you need help.' With personal problems, he implied.

'No,' I said. 'No problems of that kind.' For, of course, I had immediately sensed the Buchmanite approach.

'Oh well,' he said, getting up, 'think it over. There's a meeting next Tuesday. If you can come along, you'll be welcome and I'll introduce you to the Doctor.'

'Thanks,' I said, as I showed him out of the door.

This was a dull beginning to a fateful day. I don't know if it had any connection with my, otherwise inexplicable, sudden decision to give a party.

I was extremely worried about money, and in a week's time I would become legally liable for my own debts. It was an act of insanity, at this moment, to incur further liabilities. My battels (the college bursar's bill for all the good things I had consumed during the previous term) remained unpaid. Nevertheless, I have to record that, in defiant mood, I went round to James Brown, my wine merchant, and ordered four crates of beer and a case of sherry. From the wine merchant's, I telephoned three friends who would, I knew, pass the word round without further prompting, that there would be a jazz-record session in my rooms from early afternoon onwards. Then I went back to the college to await the arrival of my crates and prepare a three-foot-high pile of records, mostly Brunswick, in some sort of order of play for whoever wanted to be disc jockey.

I opened a bottle of sherry, poured myself a large glass and relaxed in my armchair before the fire. When I woke up, there were already fifteen people in the room, swooning around to a particularly loud version of 'St James Infirmary Blues'. Both beer and sherry were in generous circulation. Through the noise of the music I could hear some sharp knocking sounds on my ceiling, which obviously came from the room above. I ignored this, and began to join in the carouse.

A few minutes later, Saunders, the under-porter from the lodge, popped his head round my door and said, 'Mr Brown Brown's compliments, sir, and the noise from your rooms is interfering with his work. If it doesn't stop, he will have to complain to the Dean.'

'Thank you, Saunders,' I said. 'I'll do my best.'

My best, however, was not enough. Though I could suppress the voices of the loudest men in the room, the turning-off of the gramophone was quite another matter. About ten minutes later there was a firm knock at the door, and Buller, the college porter, majestic of mien, an ex-beefeater from the Tower of London, looked in.

'The Dean's compliments, sir, and will you go to see him at once.'

'Certainly, Buller. Thank you,' I said.

78

I looked around for my gown, found it, and went round to the Dean's rooms. The Dean, his pipe tilted upwards from the corner of his mouth, said simply, 'Lassalle, you will clear your rooms in the next half-hour.'

'Yes, sir,' I said. But, on my way back to my rooms, I saw to my horror that a procession – a kind of second echelon of guests, including five or six very pretty girls; clearly, from their blonde auras, Scandinavian – was already moving towards my staircase. These reinforcements had also very obviously lunched extremely well, and were under the leadership of 'Bones' Astley, who was now showing them up the staircase, and they were about to debouch into my already overcrowded rooms.

Inside, 'Bones' at once opened the windows, to provide the ladies of the party with fresh air. This was a shrewd move on his part, for immediately four pretty ladies leant out over the windowsills and were sick on to the flowerbeds below.

Imagine my predicament. How was I to clear the rooms? Although the gramophone had been turned down, the vocal noise was now as loud as that of an angry football crowd. Through the din, for the second time, I heard the majestic Buller. He was saying, 'The Dean's compliments, sir, and will you clear your rooms at once.' But he spoke in vain . . .

When I returned from Greece in 1936 and, a year later, took over a music publishing company in which an imprudent relative of mine had made an inadequate investment, I found myself, as a lover of fish and jazz, in a uniquely appropriate tactical position. My offices in Old Compton Street were situated only a hundred yards away from Wheeler's original oyster bar and only two doors away from the Swiss Hotel (as the Helvetia pub was then called). Both of these establishments supplied fine hot and cold shellfish dishes at lunchtime. My visits to Wheeler's became an almost daily routine, and the Swiss Hotel was very soon a mere extension of my office.

Down the road – again about a hundred yards – was the musicians' slave market in Archer Street. Here, daily, there gathered some fifty or sixty hack instrumentalists who put themselves on offer for single jobs, one-night bookings or 'gigs'. The fees offered to these slaves of the muse – whether jazz or classical – ran from six to ten guineas a night.

There were other topographical advantages to the office for, in a first-floor room immediately opposite us, a beautiful black teenager called Milly was just setting herself up in business for the first time. She was a delightful girl, and generous to a fault, often, drawing back her curtains at crucial moments and allowing us splendid insights into the mysteries of her fledgling enterprise.

Though my catalogue was extremely small, I was trying to upgrade it. Spencer Williams, the composer of 'Basin Street Blues', was one of those on my list. Fela Sowande, a fine musician, was my arranger. But my office rapidly became more of a club than a place of business. Old friends from Oxford days soon found me out.

Tony Spurgin was the first: skilled in the mysteries of percussion – in other words, a drummer. Drummers have always been thought of as particularly liable to neurosis of one kind and another. Tony, in his modest career, did nothing to dilute this corporate image.

Spurgin played drums with the Arthur Young Swing Sextet in Hatchetts, Piccadilly, opposite the Ritz. This group included Denis Moonan, Eugene Pini and Stephane Grappelli. When I first met Grappelli, he was, according to rumour, a very sick man indeed, with not long to live. Tuberculosis was the disease of which he was supposed to be dying, so when I met him my eyes were moist with sympathy. (Fifty years later, I am still listening with astonishment to the wizardry of his fingering.) Grappelli's accession to the band immediately made Hatchetts a place to go to.

(Much later, during the first blitz on London, as air-raid warnings alternated with the all-clear sirens in quick succession and the adrenalin was in continuous flow, the spice of danger on the dance floor in a crowded Hatchetts was enhanced by the bravura joint travesty of the wailing sirens performed by Grappelli and Pini together, *fortissimo* on their bell-toned fiddles. Coming out of Hatchetts late one night, when Grappelli and Pini were insulting Goering's Luftwaffe with their wild siren-howl, I was the privileged spectator of a unique feat of evasive athleticism. Across the road from Hatchetts, a policeman became aware that a stick of bombs was descending somewhere in his immediate neighbourhood. Reckoning that it was heading for the Ritz itself, he started running, full pelt, along the pavement in the direction of St

James's churchyard. At all costs, he must get as far as possible from the Ritz before that stick dropped. Suddenly it became brilliantly and instantly clear to him that the furious whining of trajectiles above him indicated without any doubt that the falling stick of bombs would straddle that very churchyard towards which he was travelling as fast as his legs would carry him. It was only a matter of microseconds before he began to reverse his direction and, striking sparks from his boots, skidded in a narrow circle, redoubled his speed, his arms flailing like oars, and regained the shelter of the broad pillars of the Ritz arcade just as the bombs fell across the churchyard, Piccadilly and Coventry Street. (Was it that night, I try now to recollect, that the Café de Paris was hit, destroying, apart from many customers, 'Snakehips' Johnson and his whole band?)

I also published Denis Moonan's 'Mind, the Handel's Hot' (which later, during the war, when he had his own small regular show on the BBC, was to become his theme-song). This was a delicious pastiche of Handel in the Grappelli idiom, and marvellous to dance to.

It was early in 1939 that Fats Waller arrived in London for a recording session of his famous numbers in the Abbey Road Studios. We became very good friends, and he would use my office as his headquarters, where he would bang away at my appalling piano or, jumping up and seizing a glass of whisky, peer out of the window to see if Milly across the road was in a generous mood.

As everybody knows, Fats had a 'drink problem', and a certain amount of whisky was essential to him if he was to perform at his best, or even at all. On many occasions during his recording sessions, I would receive an urgent call from the studios, rush out, buy a half-bottle of Scotch and dispatch it to him by a heavily tipped taxi-driver.

The refuelling of Fats was only one of his problems. He was once refused entrance to the Café Royal. This infuriated him, not so much on account of the personal racial insult, but because he had been prevented from listening to the saccharine melodies played by Haidee de Rance's Ladies' String Quartet.

I took over Smoky Joe's, a small basement nightclub in Gerrard Street, in order to give Fats a farewell party. When he left London, he took with him a song composed by Spencer Williams for me, called 'All Pent Up in a Penthouse', which he undertook to exploit in the United States. Nothing came of this, and the plates of the music itself were destroyed when my premises in Old Compton Street were obliterated by a bomb during the war . . .

Jazz mime

My own personal exercises in jazz mime are exceedingly simple, needing only the initial stimulus of one of my favourite tunes. I am particularly attached to 'Honeysuckle Rose', from a tape of Grappelli or Fats Waller. As soon as the melody hits my ear, movement begins with a simple swinging of my arms around my body, fitting myself, as it were, into the rhythm. After a few minutes of this mild warming-up procedure, my hips join in with the swinging arms. Almost at once, preening begins, and I am already back in memory either at the Old Parsonage or in my rooms at 'Wuggins' where the forceful voice of Buller is saying, 'Clear your rooms, sir.' Or I may be listening to Fats Waller in the Nest – a London nightclub central to the jazz scene in the 1930s – as he jumps up and down on the piano stool, his hands fluttering over the keys. Or perhaps I am in Smoky Joe's, watching Milly of Old Compton Street flirting outrageously with Fats, to absolutely no avail . . .

Every muscle in my body is now in unforced natural motion, with an immediate tonic effect.

Here in Cyprus, this kind of exercise is best performed after a good fish lunch and a modicum of good wine. If guests are present, which is often the case, the showing-off, peacocking element of jazz mime soon appears. Though this may occasion a few laughs, the peacocking feature of jazz mime is important. It acts to remove all those inhibitions which tend to clog the ageing mind and slow the ageing body. A measure of conceit or self-approbation is a stimulus to the brain, and we should not be too shy to display it.

After a period of jazz mime, I invariably sense an improvement in the circulation of the blood throughout my body. Then it is time for a few hours' siesta of deeply satisfying sleep.

Marching

For the origin of march mime, I have to go back to my second Infantry training course at the Royal Sussex Regiment detachment at Arundel. I was in the washroom of my billet, blancoing my webbing equipment for the third time in two days, when an angel disguised as a training-sergeant addressed me sharply: 'You, Lassalle, get changed into clean fatigues and report to Major Norfolk in the detachment offices.'

I was not conscious of having recently committed any military crime, so that when I knocked on the orderly-room door, I was not actually quaking with fear. 'Come in,' said a voice not notably military or severe.

I entered, saluted, and said, '6409151, Private Lassalle, sir.'

'Ah,' said the voice from behind a trestle table. 'I see, Lassalle, from your papers, that you have an Honours degree.'

'Yes, sir,' I said. 'Not a very good one.'

'It entitles me to believe that you can read and write, I suppose?'

'Certainly read and write, sir.'

'How good are you on a typewriter?'

'Oh, not bad, sir,' I lied manfully.

'Well,' said Major Norfolk, 'you're just the fellow I've been looking for.'

So, as an orderly-room clerk and occasional messenger, I began a short period of happiness in the cushiest job that ever fell to my lot in two years in the ranks. It was too good to last, and suddenly, as I was just over six feet tall, had no known criminal record and could read and write, I was without ceremony posted to Mytchett Camp in Hampshire for Military Police training. At Mytchett, ceremonial drill under giant sergeants from the Guards' Regiments was the main feature of the six-week course.

My own squad came under a magnificent, mustachioed Sergeant Organ, who began by hammering us into shape through the sheer thunder of his voice, edged with wounding mockery. But as we advanced in drill efficiency his ferocity fell from him and he became for us more and more the impresario, until, by the time the end of our course came in sight, Sergeant Organ's squad could be described as a thoroughly professional company of ritual military performers. He appealed to our vanity, calling for 'bags of swank, gentlemen', and we gave it to him in full measure, particularly in the slow march, with the magnificent opportunities it offered for self-exhibition and swank at the 'About turn'. Although members of other squads would occasionally refer to us as 'Sergeant Organ's Ballet Girls', and cast doubt on our virility, we nevertheless won the squad drill competition in our passing-out parade on completion of our course.

March mime

Both the quick march and the slow should be practised every morning before breakfast for twenty minutes. In our house in Cyprus, the distance from our front door to the end wall of the veranda is approximately forty-five yards, and this becomes my imaginary Mytchett parade ground where, each time I come to that 'About turn', I can clearly hear Sergeant Organ's exhortatory, 'Hup, hup, hup! Get those knees up now. Bags of swank, gentlemen!' Sergeant Organ always addressed us as if we were officer cadets, a subtle touch of his which endeared him to us all.

Games and sports mime

We all have our favourite sports, whether we have taken part in them or merely watched them as spectators. Any incident that has left a deep impression on the mind may be revived and relived through mime practice initiated by creative nostalgia.

In my own case, cricket and certain cricketers are the sources on which I draw. My father was a very keen follower of cricket, and in my boyhood, whenever he was on leave, he would try to watch as many matches as he could. His favourite team was Kent, and in that team his favourite player was a bowler named Frank Woolley. Somehow the image of that bowler and his great elegance of style has always remained clearly impressed on my mind. Tall himself – perhaps six foot – he would, when he raised his arm up high before bowling, seem to double in stature. Then with casual approach, not nearly as slow as it appeared, he would bring the ball down sharply from its great height to hit the ground, spinning one way or the other exactly where he wanted it, and this he could repeat with astonishing regularity for perhaps two hours on end, without perceptibly lagging or any loss of accuracy in delivery.

After my (miraculous) cure of arthritis, I adopted the mime of this action of Woolley's as a regular exercise, perhaps to emphasise the completeness of my recovery from that disability. Other sporting events do not seem to spur me to action in mime, as they will spur various readers, I am sure. But the rehearsal in my mind of past events such as Father Cyril casting at daisies on the lawn at Ross-on-Wye, and myself dapping with 'daddies' for trout on Lough Corrib, are constant aids, when I am restless, to deep and invigorating sleep.

5
PLEASURES OF FISH
At Home and Abroad

In the places I have visited in the course of a long life, mostly in Europe and the Middle East, I have been able to enjoy many of their characteristic fish dishes. In the recipes which follow, an idiosyncratic attempt is made to recall and record for the reader some of the best of those happy prandial experiences. (There are also recipes in which I embody what seem to me appropriate fantasies of my own.)

Unlike the recipes given in my regimen which, though intentionally highly flavoured, may be considered essentially austere, some of those which follow are rich in ingredients which are now frowned on by dieticians. However, in my opinion, not only should great cooking traditions be preserved – and what better way of preserving them than reviving them in one's own kitchen? – but also surely we do not want, as some (there are more and more of them; it seems like a new religion) would have it, to live in order to be healthy, but to be healthy in order to live. Occasional festive indulgences are what distinguish the happy worldling from the sombre anchorite obsessively fasting in his cave.

===

All the recipes that follow are for four people unless otherwise indicated.

The British Isles

It has always seemed to me that English cooking, at its best, has two qualities: the gentle and the sturdy. These can of course, as anyone eating out in England will have observed, degenerate into the insipid and the coarse (as exemplified, for instance, by tasteless, over-cooked vegetables and a too lavish use of bad-quality malt vinegar). But increasingly nowadays we can rejoice in dishes whose natural flavours are only subtly enhanced, allowed to speak for themselves, or whose forthright qualities command our admiration.

It is a source of regret to me that there is an absence of any fish-soup tradition in English cookery. When I come to prepare an English fish menu, I must seek elsewhere for the first course. The one that immediately springs to my mind is whitebait.

WHITEBAIT

In his delightful book, *The Vicomte in the Kitchen* (1933), the Vicomte de Mauduit writes as follows:

> During his visits to England, M. Briand used to say after each dish of whitebait (and every day he spent in London he ate whitebait) that only in the English capital could he find the best whitebait.
>
> Politicians seem to be true gourmets, at any rate in the matter of whitebait. Was not Mr Gladstone a frequent guest at the whitebait dinners which Sir Henry Irving used to launch as a great form of feast at Greenwich?
>
> Whitebait are indeed delicious – the Thames whitebait in particular, which have the finest flavour of any – and they have, besides, the distinction of carrying with them the only exception where the rule about red wine and fish does not follow. With whitebait the old custom of drinking mulled claret must be adhered to.

Here the Vicomte and I part company. I have never agreed with that inflexible rule about the incompatibility of red wine and fish, but our attitudes have changed since Swift wrote:

> They say fish should swim thrice:
> First it should swim in the sea,
> Then it should swim in butter
> And, at last, sirrah, it should swim in good claret.

I feel no compulsion to accompany whitebait with claret (especially when *mulled*).

Whitebait should not be washed: if freshly caught, they should be put to drain for about half an hour before cooking. They should then be gently shaken up with flour, until coated, in a cloth or a paper bag, and put straight – without being handled – into very hot oil or fat, and fried until crisp (for about 1½ minutes). The Vicomte suggests they should be served with a *Sauce Tartare* to which *un soupçon* of garlic has been added, but I think that all they need is salt, black pepper and a squeeze of lemon juice. Serve with brown bread and butter.

For four people, 675g (1½lb) whitebait should suffice.

KEDGEREE

This is one of my favourite dishes, and I like it in its gentlest, most English form. I read somewhere recently of a 'more Indian' version, coloured with turmeric and containing strips of chilli pepper and green ginger, and garnished with crisply fried onions. Despite a fondness for Indian food, this is not *my* kedgeree, and I do not even add a teaspoon of curry powder, loosened with 25g (1oz) melted butter – as many people do – to my version.

450g (1lb) smoked haddock

milk to cover

200g (7oz) long-grain rice

3 hard-boiled eggs, chopped

1 dessertspoon finely chopped parsley

1 dessertspoon finely ground black pepper

100g (4oz) melted butter

Poach the haddock in sufficient milk just to cover for 6 minutes, then fillet and flake it. Boil the rice for 12½ minutes. Drain well, and dry out, under a cloth or a layer of kitchen paper in the bottom of a very low oven (Gas 2/150°C/300°F). Every grain should be separated. Now mix in the fish and all the other ingredients, distributing them evenly throughout the rice with a wide-pronged fork. Cover and make very hot in the preheated low oven.

To me – though many varieties of fresh white fish can be used in kedgeree – flakes from the head and tail remaining from a fresh salmon (or, at a pinch, boned and flaked tinned salmon) are the only really acceptable substitutes for haddock.

I should mention that there is a powerful school of thought – to which I do not belong – which believes that a kedgeree should be 'creamy'. If this is your view, follow the recipe above but, at the last minute, add 1–2 beaten eggs *or* 2–3 tablespoons of cream, and cook for just 1 minute more.

FISH CAKES

Serves 4–6

A breakfast dish, I have always thought, only rivalled by kedgeree or a kipper – and fish cakes have the advantage over kedgeree that they can be prepared in advance, the day before, and will only require a short period of shallow frying at a time when many people feel disinclined for much cooking. But, accompanied by grilled tomatoes and a green vegetable, they're also good for lunch or supper.

Salmon is my favourite ingredient for fishcakes, but haddock runs it a close second. However, almost any variety of cooked fish can be used, and so can tinned salmon and tuna (if canned in oil, drain and rinse before using).

450g (1lb) cooked and flaked fish
450g (1lb) potato, mashed with 25g (1oz) butter, but no milk
1 egg, separated
1 tablespoon finely chopped parsley
salt and freshly ground black pepper
breadcrumbs
50g (2oz) butter *or* oil for frying

Thoroughly mix together the fish and mashed potato. Add the beaten egg yolk, parsley and seasoning. Cool the mixture as necessary; then, on a floured board, form it into 6–8 flat cakes. Turn these in the whisked egg white, and then coat with breadcrumbs. Shallow fry till golden brown, turning once.

This is a very gentle mixture. A tablespoon of chopped chives and/or a teaspoon of creamed horseradish and/or a teaspoon of anchovy essence can be added if you desire more 'zing'.

FISH CUSTARD

Moments of languor occur in the lives of even the healthiest and most ichthyophagous of us. Perhaps we are convalescing from some illness; or perhaps there has been a recent tendency towards excess. At such times, this recipe should surely be a source of calm and refreshment.

450g (1lb) white fish fillets, rolled
3 eggs
450ml (¾ pint) milk
¼ teaspoon salt
a sprinkling of nutmeg

Arrange the fillets in a fireproof dish. Beat the eggs lightly in a mixing bowl. Add the milk and seasonings. Pour the mixture over the rolled fillets and bake in a moderate oven (Gas 4/ 180 °C/350°F) for 45 minutes.

This dish can also be made with leftover white fish, flaked.

Fish with bacon

From the delicacy and refinement of the Fish Custard, I now feel impelled to make a vigorous leap towards that English tradition to which I have such an ambivalent attitude: the combination of fish with bacon.

Elvers, the 'Whitebait of the West', the tiny eels which appear in the River Severn in Gloucestershire in the early spring, are traditionally fried in bacon fat. Scallops and bacon (also cooked in France as *Coquilles Saint-Jacques en Brochette*) are a favourite with many people and are a speciality of my beloved Manzi's Restaurant in Soho★ (though it is my wife, rather than I, who tends to order this dish). By the way, I am glad that alligator is not a fish, for if it were I might feel compelled to order it at Manzi's who are now offering their customers alligator steaks from Florida.

SCALLOPS AND BACON

Two small scallops should suffice per person

---

scallops

---

half a rasher of the very best bacon, so
finely cut that it is almost transparent,
for each piece of scallop

Maître d'Hôtel (Parsley) Butter
(see page 207)

Remove and discard the 'skirt' (the straggling grey edge which surrounds the scallop). Cut the main white body of the scallop into two parts, vertically. Detach the coral roe, and reserve.

Stretch each half-rasher of your ultra-fine bacon and roll it round a portion of scallop, securing it with a toothpick. Alternate each of these wrapped and skewered portions of scallop with a

---

★1 Leicester Street, London WC2 (tel. 01–734 0224/5).

small portion of the roe, on a skewer. Brush with melted *Maître d'Hôtel* Butter and put under a hot grill for 6 minutes on either side, basting all the while with the Butter.

Remove the toothpicks and serve on the skewers, with lemon quarters.

The following recipe, collected by Florence White in Lancashire, and included in her *Good Things in England* (1932), is a more unusual one.

BAKED WHITE FISH, BACON AND GREEN PEAS

'Sea bream, fresh haddocks, rock salmon, codlings, fillets, etc, can all be made into a savoury nourishing dish if put into a brown baking dish, floured and covered with rashers of bacon (or some breadcrumbs or bits of butter or clarified beef dripping may be sprinkled over the fish, and the rashers of bacon can be rolled and placed along each side). The dish is then baked in a good oven and will be done in about half an hour.

'Bacon with fish is a favourite dish with fisherfolk, and at Blackpool green peas are always served with it.'

WHITE FISH FLAN

I have never been an admirer of the fish pie covered with pastry as opposed to mashed potato. However, a good fish flan is another matter. I specify 'good' to avoid any association with the ubiquitous cold so-called 'quiches' - the pastry either rock-hard or soggy – which have, of recent years in England, proliferated everywhere from pubs to school catering departments.

for shortcrust pastry

150g (6oz) plain flour

a pinch of salt

75g (3oz) butter

25g (1oz) shortening

1 egg yolk

1–2 tablespoons water

for the filling

25g (1oz) butter

150g (6oz) finely sliced onions

1 dessertspoon plain flour

150ml (¼ pint) milk

salt and pepper

a large pinch of grated nutmeg

2 eggs, beaten

3 tomatoes

225g (8oz) cooked and flaked white fish
25g (1oz) Parmesan cheese, grated
25g (1oz) Gruyère cheese, grated

Sift the flour and salt into a mixing bowl. Cut the butter and shortening in small pieces, into the flour, until they are well coated. Rub in with the fingers till the mixture has the texture of fine breadcrumbs. Mix the egg yolk with the water, tip into the flour and fat, and mix quickly with a palette knife until you have a firm dough. Turn on to a floured board and knead lightly until smooth. Chill for at least half an hour before using.

Place the flan ring (or a loose-bottomed sandwich-cake tin can be used) on a baking sheet. Roll out the pastry to a diameter about 3.5cm (1½in) bigger than the flan ring. Lift the pastry into the flan ring, quickly easing it down. Press the pastry gently into the shape of the ring. Now bend back the top edge and cut off the excess pastry. Chill again for about half an hour. Line the pastry with crumpled greaseproof paper and three-quarters fill the flan with uncooked beans to retain the shape. (The beans can be used many times over for this purpose.) Bake blind for 20 minutes at Gas 6/ 200°C/400°F, after which take the flan out of the oven and carefully remove the paper and beans. Replace the flan in the oven for another 6 minutes. When baked, slide the flan on to a wire rack and leave to cool.

Now heat the butter. When it has melted, add the onions and soften till they are transparent (they should not brown). Mix in the flour and allow to cook for 1 minute. Add the milk, stirring until boiling. Remove the pan from the heat. Add the seasoning and nutmeg, and the beaten eggs. Scald, peel and halve the tomatoes, and remove the seeds. Arrange them, cut side down, with the fish on the base of the flan. Season well and pour on the sauce. Sprinkle the top with the cheeses. Bake for 20–25 minutes, until well set and golden brown, at an oven temperature of Gas 5/190°C/375°F.

Three sauces

It was Voltaire who said that the English have a hundred religions but only one sauce. I have always wondered which one he was talking about. Some people say it was bread sauce. It could have been oyster sauce or one of the many sauces made with claret as early as the seventeenth century. It could have been apple or caper sauce. (English housewives pickled nasturtium seeds as an excellent substitute for capers.) Voltaire was unfair . . .

Sauces have the same tendency as other English dishes to be either mild or forceful. I give an example of each.

EGG SAUCE

This is based on the essential *Béchamel*.

50g (2oz) butter
50g (2oz) plain flour
900ml (1½ pints) milk
1 medium onion, chopped finely
bouquet garni of thyme, parsley and bay leaf
¼ teaspoon salt
½ teaspoon freshly ground black pepper
3 hard-boiled eggs

In a saucepan, melt the butter and add the flour, to make a *roux;* pour on the milk slowly, stirring constantly, and bring to simmering point. Add the onions, herbs and seasonings and cook slowly for up to 30 minutes. Remove the *bouquet garni.*

Chop each egg into eight pieces, and add to the *Béchamel.* (I suppose, as we are being so English, we should refer to this as 'white' sauce.)

Egg sauce makes a pleasing accompaniment to any grilled fish. For English people, it seems always to have had a special affinity with cod.

MUSTARD SAUCE

300ml (½ pint) *Béchamel* ('white') sauce,
as in previous recipe

1 heaped teaspoon English mustard
powder, made up with tarragon vinegar

1 dessertspoon chilli vinegar

½ teaspoon anchovy essence

Remove the *Béchamel* from the stove and stir in the other ingredients. This is particularly good with herrings, grilled or fried with a coating of oatmeal.

PORTOBELLO SAUCE

Although this sauce is featured (largely) in *The Adventurous Fish Cook,* I cannot resist repeating it here as it is, I feel, perhaps my one claim to immortality. Whenever I have produced it, it has been greeted with acclaim, and I was pleased to hear from a London gourmet friend that he 'makes it up in batches'. It contains many foreign ingredients, and its sole claim to be English rests on my having invented it.

---

12 large black Kalamata olives

---

1 small ripe avocado pear

---

2 cloves garlic

---

4 anchovy fillets

---

juice of ½ lemon

150ml (¼ pint) dry red wine

150ml (¼ pint) olive oil

---

1 teaspoon freshly ground black pepper

---

2 egg yolks

---

for garnish

---

1 tablespoon red sweet pepper, finely chopped

Stone the olives and pound them with the flesh of the avocado, the two cloves of garlic and the anchovy fillets. Add the lemon juice and the wine and put through the blender. Now put the mixture in a small, heavy saucepan, add the olive oil and cook for 7 or 8 minutes, stirring well. Season with the freshly ground black pepper. To the well-beaten egg yolks, in a mixing bowl, gradually

98

add the *cooled* mixture, beating with a wooden spoon. This sauce can also be served hot, in which case put it in a double saucepan or a *bain-marie* and stir over a gentle heat. Garnish – hot or cold – with the finely chopped red pepper.

This sauce is excellent with fish of strong flavour: skate, conger, dogfish, monkfish, porbeagle, tunny, squid and octopus. The fish can be grilled, or poached in a fish stock (see page 113). Cold, it makes a delicious dip, to be eaten with chunks of good bread.

Savouries

I have noticed an almost mystical illogic in one aspect of menu selection in England, both in restaurants and in private houses. My wife, on a recent visit to California – home of the health fanatic and temple of the cult of the body beautiful – observed the same phenomenon.

First courses are light and fresh. The main course – whether of fish, poultry or lean meat – is never fried. Vegetables are briefly cooked and never smothered in butter, while the potato is almost wholly eschewed. A salad is an obligatory constituent of nearly every meal.

Then comes the pudding or sweet – the 'dessert' in the United States – and all pretence of healthy eating is abandoned. Cholesterol-high concoctions are the rule. Butter-rich *gâteaux* and pastries are served forth; cream and chocolate abound. My wife describes how, in a Los Angeles restaurant, after oysters followed by salmon salad, the company – including her – partook of casings of solid chocolate, filled to the brim with flavoured cream. You will see the same procedure being followed in London every night of the week.

Fresh fruit is, of course, the obvious alternative. (In Cyprus, this is the only sweet course available in most restaurants.) But it can pall, and – particularly when one is entertaining guests – one sometimes feels the urge for something more festive. I suggest that the answer lies in a renascence of the savoury: as an alternative – *not* a follow-on to the sweet course.

'In England this term [the savoury] describes a range of light preparations. Served right at the end of dinner, even after dessert, these might be called *post-oeuvre* as distinct from *hors-d'oeuvre*, served at the beginning of the meal.'

So *Larousse Gastronomique*; and in 1933 the Vicomte de Mauduit was saying pretty much the same thing in *The Vicomte in the Kitchen*: 'Savouries are essentially an English dish, and are to the English what *hors-d'oeuvre* are to the French, only backwards, in the sense that *hors-d'oeuvre* begin a French meal, and savouries end the English dinner.'

In 1956, Constance Spry wrote of the after-dinner savoury: 'This course, which used inevitably to follow the sweet course in my young days, sometimes now takes the place of this, particularly for those whose taste lies in a savoury direction.'

All the same, ever since the beginning of the Second World War, savouries had been on their way out. Now, the after-dinner (or let us call it 'end-of-dinner') savoury is almost extinct, except on the menus of banquets and grand official dinners where, in the old style, it follows the sweet course.

What were the origins of this quintessentially English end-of-dinner course (see Lady Jekyll's comment on the French reaction to it, on page 103)? The first reference to it I can find is in Eliza Acton's *Modern Cookery* (1845). She describes 'Savoury Toasts' which she says may be served 'in the cheese-course of a dinner'. She adds, 'Such mere "relishes", as they are called, do not seem to us to demand much of our space, or many of them which are very easy of preparation might be inserted here: a good cook, however, will easily supply them at slight expense.'

This is not the place to discuss the intricacies of Victorian menus. Suffice it to say that in the original *Mrs Beeton* (1861), a dinner normally consisted of a first course (soup and fish), an *entrée* ('made-up' dishes such as fricassées, rissoles, *vols-au-vent*, and so on), a second course (meat and roast poultry) and a third course under which heading was lumped a – to us – extraordinary assortment of dishes (for instance, on one dinner menu, or 'bill of fare' as Mrs Beeton calls it: Ducklings, Tartlets of Strawberry Jam, Cheesecakes, *Gâteau de Riz*, Carrot Pudding, Sea-kale). This was followed by dessert (fruit and nuts, sometimes accompanied by cakes and biscuits).

Lurking among the dishes in the third course, those cheesecakes will have caught your eye. In other menus, you will find in their place such dishes as Brillat-Savarin's Fondue and Macaroni with Parmesan Cheese. In the menus for plain family dinners, however, you will note that a third course sometimes consists of plain cheese.

Mrs Beeton, like Eliza Acton, speaks of a 'cheese course' ('Rusks, cheese-biscuits, pats or slices of butter, and salad, cucumber or water-cresses, should always form part of a cheese course.'), and under cover of this category (part of the third course) the savoury crept in. In one of the recipes Mrs Beeton gives for this course, the anchovy appears. This recipe, for Scotch Woodcock (I give a version of it on page 106) includes *no cheese*.

From such modest beginnings, the savoury was by the end of the last century to have risen to individual prominence and glory. In *Menus Made Easy* by Nancy Lake (9th edition, 1899), which is subtitled 'How to Order Dinner and Give the Dishes their French Names', it has become a course on its own, the 'Savoury Entremets', which follows the 'Entremets' (the sweet course). The dishes listed here include all sorts of little pastries, mousses and various concoctions containing ham, *foie gras* and other ingredients apart from cheese (but the majority of them are based on fish).

The fifteenth edition of *Savouries à la Mode* by Mrs de Salis was published in 1896. In her preface to this charming little book, Mrs de Salis says, 'Savoury dishes at the present time being so fashionable, and novelties in them so much inquired for, I have been persuaded by my friends to publish a small book on the subject.'

My own feeling is that this tremendous popularity of the savoury was much influenced by Edward VII (first as Prince of Wales and then as King). He was especially fond of savoury – as opposed to sweet – dishes. (Indeed, hostesses who were expecting him to tea would always provide lobster salad in addition to the vast obligatory spread of sandwiches, scones, little cakes, big cakes, and so on.) One of Mrs de Salis's recipes is named after him:

PRINCE OF WALES
CANAPÉS
Canapés à la Prince de Galles

'Take some fine prawns, fillets of anchovies, celery, two gherkins, and two truffles. Cut all these into small squares, put them into a basin with enough Prince of Wales sauce to season the ingredients. Fill ramequin or china cases with this mixture, and lay a piece of aspic jelly on the top of each, garnishing with the same chopped.

'Prince of Wales sauce for above: two yolks of eggs boiled hard, two anchovies, some tarragon, the latter parboiled and dried, a few capers, a little mustard and the yolk of an egg. Bruise all these in a mortar, and then work in one tablespoonful of salad oil, a teaspoonful of tarragon vinegar, and rub through a sieve.'

The elaboration of this recipe (especially the truffles and aspic) suit it better to the opulent era of the savoury's heyday than to our own. However, in encouraging a revival of the savoury, I can suggest many more appropriate and simpler alternatives.

I should note initially that, at the height of its popularity, the savoury was frequently served on *croûtons* or slices of fried bread. These can be replaced by toast – though it is essential that this should be freshly made – or by pumpernickel or by any firm rye or wholemeal bread with the crusts removed.

ANGELS ON
HORSEBACK

This is my *beau idéal* of the savoury, on whose appearance any residual doubts I may have about the combination of fish and bacon vanish into thin air. It is also, now that oysters are so costly, a (comparatively) inexpensive way of enjoying them.

8 oysters
8 rashers very finely cut bacon
4 slices toast, with the crusts cut off

Wrap each oyster in a strip of the bacon and skewer together with a cocktail stick. Grill until the bacon is crisp. Remove the skewers, and serve two 'angels' per person, on toast.

CROÛTES AUX PRUNES FARCIES
Stuffed Prunes on Toast

Lady Jekyll, in a charming little book *Kitchen Essays* (1922), has this to say:

'The least complicated savouries are often the best, and caviare or slices of foie gras, ice-cold with hot toast, or hot truffles *en serviette* with ice-cold butter, or thin slices of smoked salmon with brown and white bread and butter are the gourmet's choice, although few fortunes or consciences are sufficiently robust in these days for luxuries so costly.'

However, for those of us with deficient fortunes or highly active consciences, she goes on to suggest, 'a novel and successful savoury . . . evolved the other day' (its French title – French names for all dishes were obligatory in those days – was obviously evolved at the same time, for, as Lady Jekyll herself remarks, the French regard a savoury course as 'something barbarous, indeed almost immoral').

'Make nice little *canapés* of fried bread [I would substitute toast], about 2 inches by 3 inches, 1 for each person; take the biggest French plum procurable (or 2), soak it and extract the stone; fill the cavity with a stuffing of Scotch dried haddock, cooked, flaked, and beaten with a little cream and red pepper to a smooth *mousse;* serve hot.'

SOFT ROES ON TOAST

Mash together ½ teaspoon of English mustard powder, ¼ teaspoon of salt and 50g (2oz) of butter. Melt in a pan, and cook soft herring roes in it gently, for 5–10 minutes, according to size. Serve piping hot on toast.

DEVILLED SOFT ROES

40g (1½oz) butter

225g (8oz) soft roes, dipped in seasoned flour

salt and black pepper for seasoning

cayenne pepper

hot toast

for garnish

lemon wedges

Place the butter in a hot pan on the stove. When it foams, put in the floured roes and dust with cayenne pepper. When brown, turn over, and repeat. Serve on toast, accompanied by lemon wedges.

SARDINES ON TOAST

Whole sardines laid out on toast, and seasoned to taste, are pleasant for family consumption. However, as a savoury course, perhaps the following has more polish.

2 × 125g (4½oz) tin sardines
2 anchovy fillets
juice of ½ lemon
few drops of Tabasco sauce *or* a pinch of cayenne pepper
freshly ground black pepper
1 teaspoon chives, chopped
1 teaspoon parsley, chopped
4 slices bread, toasted on one side only (and with crusts cut off)

Mash the sardines and the anchovy fillets. Add the other ingredients, and work into a paste. Spread this paste on the untoasted side of the bread, and grill for 5 minutes.

The bread may, optionally, be rubbed with garlic before being toasted.

A note on sardines and anchovies

Sardines and anchovies both appear in the above recipe, and anchovies in the following one. In recipes for savouries, tinned sardines and anchovies come into their own. This is one case where, both in texture and flavour, the tinned product is preferable to the fresh. However, I beg you to study the inscriptions on the tins in which you buy both these fish. Sardines should be tinned in *olive* oil, and anchovies should be ...

anchovies. Close inspection of many brands of so-called anchovies reveals that they are actually 'anchovied fillets of sardine'. These are inferior in both taste and texture.

SCOTCH WOODCOCK

Florence White (in *Good Things in England*) tells us that this recipe is from a Suffolk manuscript cookery book and that its date is the second quarter of the nineteenth century. She remarks that 'its contents represent very definitely the extremely good English cookery of that period'. I agree, and though some may complain that its cholesterol content is high, after all it is intended for four people.

'Ingredients:
bread 4 slices; anchovies 7 or 8; eggs 4; cream ½ pint [300ml]; pepper and salt; [butter].

time: about 30 minutes all told.

Method
1 Toast the bread and butter well on both sides.

2 Wash and scrape and chop the anchovies and spread them between two slices of toast.

3 Have ready the yolks of the eggs well beaten with the cream and seasoned with cayenne pepper and salt.

4 Set them over the fire to thicken but don't let them boil.

5 Pour over the toast and send to table as hot as possible.

NB The expense of this dish may be lessened by using the whole of the eggs and beating them up with ¼ pint of milk (and, if you have it, a *little* cream) but of course it won't be *quite* so good, and as in some houses and places cream is plentiful the original is given as it stands.'

I strongly recommend that the original should be followed.

MUSHROOMS WITH
ANCHOVY CREAM

Florence White identifies this as a Cambridge college recipe of 1881. I would note that toast could be substituted for the fried bread, but again I give the recipe in its original form.

'Ingredients:
rounds of bread about 2 inches across; mushrooms; anchovies 9 or 10; cream 1 or 2 tablespoonfuls; pepper; salt.

Method
1 Cut some rounds of bread about ¼ inch thick and 2 inches in diameter.

2 Fry them a golden brown.

3 Broil some mushrooms and put one on each piece of fried bread.

4 Wash 9 or 10 anchovies.

5 Chop them.

6 Rub them through a sieve.

7 Whip the cream.

8 Mix the anchovies with it, season with a little pepper and salt.

9 Just before sending to table put a piece of this mixture about the size of a walnut on each mushroom and serve.'

Note: Obviously the mushrooms used in the above recipe should be the flat, flavourful brown kind – not the 'buttons' – and in no circumstances should they be tinned.

TARAMA WITH TOAST

Tarama is Greek (the recipe for it is given on page 131). However, I make no apology for including it here. It is the savoury *course* which is English and I see no reason why foreign dishes should not make their appearance in it if they are suited to its requirements.

Serve the *Tarama* with hot toast and lemon quarters. Let the guests help themselves, as they do with pâtés.

Other suggestions for savouries

The field of savoury-making offers plenty of opportunity for creative innovation. I would refer you to the *Coquilles* section of my chapter on first courses (page 210).

Scallop-shells are too big for savouries, though the smaller pyrex and white ovenware reproductions of them can be used; so can little pyrex or ovenware ramekins.

All the suggestions made for *Coquilles* can be followed here – with two provisos. Firstly, I would not recommend a mashed-potato topping for a savoury; it is too substantial. Secondly, the essence of the savoury course is that its seasoning should be vigorous. Rich, bland variations of the *Béchamel* (such as Cream Sauce) are not suitable. When making savoury with *Béchamel,* you could use any of the following additions, just before mixing in the fish. The quantities suggested are for 300ml (½ pint) *Béchamel* (see pages 96, 161 and 162).

1 teaspoon curry paste
1 dessertspoon anchovy essence *or* 50g (2oz) Anchovy Butter (see page 208)
1 dessertspoon horseradish cream
1–2 tablespoons red lumpfish roe
1 teaspoon Dijon mustard

Cooked, flaked or minced fish can be heated with a pat of the savoury butter of your choice (see pages 207–8) and then spread on toast and finished off under the grill. (Smoked haddock is particularly good prepared in this way.) Garnish with a little finely chopped parsley and some freshly ground black pepper.

Note: Perhaps it is unnecessary to state that, apart from its piquant flavour, the savoury course has one other essential: it must be *hot*. A cold savoury seems to me almost a contradiction in terms.

Italy

My early visits to Italy were of a religious character: a 'family audience' with the Pope on one occasion and others involving the purchase of papally-blessed rosaries to take back to England. Gastronomy was not prominent, though I remember that the food was delicious, and I was particularly struck by the fact that ice-creams were sold on the roof of Milan Cathedral. Subsequent visits were less pious – for instance my 'Holy Year' journey in 1933, as well as later holidays.

In the dark days of pre-war, wartime and post-war English cooking (a period which cuisinological historians will doubtless dub BED, ie, 'Before Elizabeth David'), and prior to the establishment of, now countless, Chinese and Indian eating-houses, one's local Italian restaurant was usually the only place where one could find decent, reasonably priced food. (This was long before the proliferation of the expensive 'interior decorator's' trattoria.) And I shall always remember with reverence Bertorelli's in Charlotte Street – still extant, I believe, though much more expensive, and mass-producing exotic up-market sorbets – with its illegible menus in purple ink and its funereally-clad, elderly and severe waitresses.

Italian cooking is probably the most regionally varied in the world, but for me, personally, it will always be essentially Mediterranean: less coarse than the Greek and less rigorous than the French. I regard it as the home of fish lyrically and polygamously wedded to tomato, garlic, olive oil and the stern and noble anchovy – as opposed to the 'anchovied fillet of sardine'.

This should not be taken to imply that I have any objection to the sardine when it appears in its true colours, either tinned in olive oil or – ideally – absolutely fresh from the sea, as it is often found on the Italian coast.

SARDE ARROSTO
Grilled fresh sardines

at least 8 fresh sardines per person

olive oil for brushing

salt and pepper

for garnish

lemon wedges

Clean the sardines and, if you wish, cut off their heads. Brush them with olive oil seasoned with salt and pepper. Grill them on each side for about 4 minutes, and serve immediately with wedges of lemon.

Depending on the quantity of sardines available, the above recipe can provide a first course or a main one. The same is true of the following dish, which can be considered as either a soup or a stew and will serve six.

BRODETTO

Serves 6

Brodetto literally means 'little broth'. In fact many people consider it the finest of all Italian fish dishes. It is a fisherman's soup, and there is a (friendly?) rivalry between various Italian Adriatic coastal towns – Venice, Ancona, Rimini, Ravenna – as to whose *brodetto* is the best. I have enjoyed it in Venice. My recipe includes fish which should be easily obtainable nowadays in northern climes.

1kg (2¼lb) assorted fish, according to availability (eg, sole, cod, mullet, whiting), cleaned and scaled
375g (12oz) squid or cuttlefish, cut into rings, and with the tentacles chopped coarsely
75g (3oz) mussels, shelled, with their juices
2 onions, coarsely chopped
2 cloves garlic, skinned and pressed
150ml (¼ pint) olive oil
450g (1lb) peeled tomatoes
1 heaped tablespoon parsley, finely chopped
salt and pepper, and a judicious sprinkling of cayenne
900ml (1½ pints) rich fish stock (see below). Make with the trimmings from the fish you are using for the soup.
1 tablespoon white wine vinegar
1 slice thick bread per person, toasted

In a large pan, cook the onions with the garlic in the olive oil until golden-brown. Add the tomatoes, parsley, salt, pepper and cayenne and cook for a few minutes, stirring constantly. Add the fish, and cook until the mixture boils. Now add the rich fish stock and wine vinegar and cook until it has reduced by one-third. Place a slice of the toasted bread in each soup bowl, and pour on the soup. Serve immediately.

RICH FISH STOCK

For this you will need to get from your fishmonger such non-oily white fish trimmings and bones as he can let you have after filleting fish. Heads and skins are also good, as are the shells of prawns. (When you ask your fishmonger to fillet a whole fish for you, always take away the 'debris' for stock.) Fish stock is used in the making of sauces and soups, as well as for the simple poaching of fish, and it is customary to make it in some quantity.

for 1¼ litres (2 pints) fish stock

1¼ litres (2 pints) water

trimmings from any non-oily fish (cod's head works wonders, as does the addition of 1 small, cleaned whiting *or* 1 small red mullet, which you need not clean)

1 large onion *or* 2 shallots, roughly chopped

the white of 1 leek, chopped

1 medium-sized carrot, chopped

1 small stick celery, chopped

thyme, parsley, fennel: a few sprigs of each are normally added (if any is un-obtainable fresh, use a pinch of the dried herb)

150ml (¼ pint) dry white wine

1 teaspoon salt

1 teaspoon ground black pepper

Put all the ingredients together in a pan. Bring to the boil, and simmer for an hour. Strain the stock and it is ready for use.

SPAGHETTI CON ACCIUGHE
Spaghetti with anchovy sauce

Though, in Italy, a pasta dish usually precedes a main course of meat or fish (the origins of this are probably economic, just as, in Cyprus, the dreaded (by me) *macaronia* – a solid mass, welded together with flour and water, dotted with fragments of mince – precedes the Sunday roast, and English farm labourers used to dull their appetite for a tiny square of bacon with a 'roly-poly' – see Flora Thompson's marvellous *Lark Rise to Candleford*), for me it is a meal, and a wonderful one, provided the pasta is fresh. This is easy to ensure nowadays, either by going to specialist pasta shops or by making your own at home. (Describing this operation is outside my province here.)

450g (1lb) spaghetti

---

6 tablespoons olive oil

---

2 large cloves garlic, crushed

---

8 anchovy fillets, pounded into a paste

---

the yolks of 3 hard-boiled eggs

---

2 tablespoons parsley, finely chopped

---

1 teaspoon freshly ground black pepper

---

juice of ½ lemon

In a large saucepan of boiling salted water, cook your spaghetti until it is just *al dente*. (This should take about 12 minutes.) With it serve the following Neapolitan sauce, either separately or, as tends to be my method, stirred in at the last moment.

Heat the oil and soften the garlic in it. Remove from the flame. To the pounded anchovies add the hard-boiled egg yolks, the parsley and the black pepper, and mash together. Stir into the oil and garlic, and reheat. Remove from the flame, and at the last minute, add the lemon juice. Toss the spaghetti in the sauce and serve immediately.

As I suggested in *The Adventurous Fish Cook,* there are many possible fishy forms of escape from the eternal spaghetti *bolognese.* Prawns, mussels or flaked tuna (fresh and cooked, or tinned) can be added to a tomato sauce, and *cannelloni* can be filled with minced or sauced fish, rather as my wife fills pancakes with the fish mixture described on page 184. (I mentioned in my previous book that I awaited only inspiration to announce the evolution of fish *ravioli.* Alas, I am still awaiting it.)

Probably the most classic Italian dish involving fish and pasta is spaghetti *alle vongole* (with clams), for which I gave a recipe in *The Adventurous Fish Cook.* I have since heard complaints that clams are not available in many places in England, and accordingly I here give a variation of that recipe in which mussels are used instead.

SPAGHETTI ALLE COZZE
Spaghetti with Mussels

450g (1lb) spaghetti

1kg (2¼lb) mussels, scraped and well rinsed in cold water

150ml (¼ pint) dry white wine

2 cloves garlic

150ml (¼ pint) olive oil

1kg (2¼lb) tomatoes, strained
1 tablespoon parsley, finely chopped
½ teaspoon coarsely ground black pepper
salt to taste

Cook the spaghetti as in the previous recipe. Place the mussels in a pan with the wine and cook until open. Remove from shells, adding the juice to the wine in the pan, and cut each mussel into four slices.

Brown the garlic in the heated olive oil. Add the mussel juice and wine, the tomatoes, parsley and pepper. Simmer for 20 minutes. Add the sliced mussels, and cook on a high flame for another minute or two. Add salt to taste. Pour sauce over spaghetti, toss and serve. (Grated cheese does not go well with this dish.)

The British, in general, have an impression that *all* Italians live on pasta. However, there is a belt of country in northern and central Italy where it is hardly ever eaten. This territory is far more suitable for growing rice and corn, the latter for *polenta* (a food which I personally can't imagine combining with fish*), than wheat. And, of course, the Italian *risotto* – in various forms – is one of the world's most delightful rice dishes.

I give here a recipe for Shrimp Risotto, taken from Ada Boni's *Talisman Italian Cook Book,* Italy's splendid standard national work on cookery.

---

*However, Alan Davidson, in *Mediterranean Seafood,* gives a recipe for cuttlefish with *polenta* which is apparently popular in the region of Venice.

RISOTTO CON GAMBERETTI
Shrimp Risotto

900g (2lb) shrimps
900ml (1½ pints) salted water
150g (6oz) butter
½ onion
1 carrot, diced finely
1 teaspoon chopped parsley
thyme
1 bay leaf
2 tablespoons cognac
1 medium onion, minced
1 tablespoon olive oil
600g (1¼lb) rice
300ml (½ pint) red wine
600ml (1 pint) stock from shells

'Shell shrimps. Boil shrimp shells for 20 minutes in salted water.

'Place 50g (2oz) butter, shrimps, onion, carrot, parsley, thyme and bay leaf in saucepan and sauté until golden brown. Add cognac and cook until evaporated.

'In another, larger pan place minced onion, olive oil and 100g (4oz) butter. Brown onion a little and add rice. Let rice brown a little, stirring frequently, then add wine. Let wine evaporate, add stock and cook until rice is tender, for about 15 minutes. Remove from heat. Pour shrimps and sauce over rice. Serves 6.'

I suppose that *gourmands* – as opposed to *gourmets* – could conceivably classify as starters the two classic Italian mix-ups – one hot, one cold – that follow. I certainly regard either as a full meal.

FRITTO MISTO
Mixed Fried Fish

I gave an iconoclastic version of this in *The Adventurous Fish Cook,* which included button mushrooms, a small sauce containing wine and capers, and a final decadent scattering of parsley. Perhaps my unorthodoxy sprang from an inescapable sense of sin. Despite the permissiveness I show in this section of the book – as opposed to in my regimen – *Fritto Misto* is the only recipe I give in which fish is *deep-fried*. I think my aversion to this method of cookery springs partly from the fact that, for many years, it was, in England, almost the *only* one used, and partly from how appallingly it was employed: oh, blanket batter . . . oh, stale, clouded oil . . . oh, so-called 'sauces'. And oh, often, under its disguise, the fish itself wearied by time and travel . . .

Fritto Misto (literally 'Mixed Fry') is, in its true incarnation, just a mixture of small, absolutely fresh fish cooked in fresh olive oil and accompanied by wedges of fresh lemon. (I am suddenly looking forward to eating it again as I did, with much relish, in Italy in younger days.)

Apparently the classic Neapolitan version consists solely of small red mullet and the bodies (cut into rings) and tentacles of tiny squid. But in Venice, soft-shell crabs and eel can be commonly found in this *fritto*. Prawns crop up in many places, so do small sardines and anchovies. Often, fillets of white fish – such as sole, young hake, monkfish – are cut into strips and included.

Obviously, when absolutely fresh fish are needed, ingredients depend on what the fisherman has caught. But equally obviously, if, for instance, you should be lucky enough to come across a haul of fresh sardines, these just won't do, on their own, in this recipe. You'll have a lovely *fritto,* but it won't be *misto.* For this dish, variety – not only of taste but of texture – is essential. It may be helpful to classify the fish needed in different groups.

118

1 **Cephalopods** Very small squid are characteristic of this dish, and you can often get them. If you can't you are unlikely to find the alternative – small cuttlefish.

2 **Shellfish** Large prawns, please, and don't remove their shells.

3 **Small fish** Very small sardines or anchovies or you could use whitebait or sprats.

4 **Larger fish** Choose sole, hake, turbot or monkfish. They should be filleted and cut into very thin strips.

5 **Red mullet** I put these last, in a category of their own, though they could well come first, being as characteristic of the dish as squid or prawns. They are caught off the English coast in the summer months, though a lot of people don't know it. Choose small ones.

Of these five categories, **3** and **4** are most easily dispensed with. You may not be able to obtain **5**, but can proceed if you have the other four. Do not dispense with the tiny squid out of cowardice: they are *not* frightening.

So now let me suggest the ingredients of a meal for four (hungry) people:

---

4 small red mullet, whole and uncleaned
(Mullet of this kind, and whitebait, are
the only fish that don't need cleaning)

8–12 large prawns, *unshelled*

300g (12oz) small squid, cleaned and
with their bodies cut into rings, and their
tentacles in separate clumps or tufts

225g (8oz) small fish (as **3** above). Unless
whitebait, they should be cleaned

225g (8oz) larger fish (as **4** above),
filleted and cut into little strips

Enough flour, seasoned with salt and
ground black pepper, for coating
(some people use batter,
but I and most Italians don't)

Enough very hot olive oil for
deep-frying (ideally, this should be
completely fresh, but olive oil can be
used up to five times, provided it is
filtered in between)★

for garnish

lemon wedges

Dip the fish into the seasoned flour just before you fry them. Cook the largest first. The mullet will take 3–5 minutes, dependent on size. The small fish will take 2–3 minutes. The prawns will take 2 minutes and so will the strips of fish. The squid, if really small, will take less than 2 minutes. Transfer each batch from the deep-frier on to kitchen paper, to drain, and then to a hot serving dish. Serve – crisp and deep gold – with lemon wedges.

INSALATA DI MARE
Seafood Salad

This is a combination of shellfish and cephalopods and can be served as a first course or as a main dish. I give quantities for a main dish that should satisfy four to six people.

The ingredients depend on availability, and here you must use your own judgment. Shellfish should predominate, but you must include a few squid or one small octopus; it would be better to use both.

★This is done by heating the oil and then pouring it through a fine sieve lined with cheesecloth or butter muslin – cf Clarified Butter, (page 167). I myself have used a coffee filter-paper for this purpose, and on one occasion a double layer of paper from an ordinary kitchen roll.

1kg (2¼lb) mussels
450g (1lb) clams (if you can't get clams, try cockles)
675g (1½lb) prawns
450g (1lb) small squid (3 or 4 squid) and/or (preferably and)
450g (1lb) octopus (1 octopus)
6 tablespoons olive oil
2 cloves garlic, peeled and crushed
2 tablespoons lemon juice
2 tablespoons parsley, finely chopped
salt and finely ground black pepper, to taste

In a heavy pan, steam open the mussels and clams. When you shell them, pour off their juices, and reserve. Boil and shell the prawns. Clean and prepare the squid and/or octopus. Cut up, bring to a boil, and then simmer until tender. (The squid won't take more than half an hour. The octopus could take up to 2 hours.) Drain and set aside.

Now, in 2 tablespoons of the olive oil, cook the crushed garlic, stirring it round until it merges. (Do not brown the garlic.) Add to the juices from the mussels and clams, and then slowly beat in the rest of the olive oil, the lemon juice, half the parsley and the seasonings. Put all your seafood (it should still be warm) into a large bowl, and mix the dressing in thoroughly. Arrange 'on a great dish' - as the Elizabethans used to say – or on individual plates (I prefer the former). Dot with the rest of the parsley.

This salad can be served chilled or tepid. (I find tepid is preferable – the flavour is stronger – unless the weather is absolutely sizzling.)

MERLUZZO IN FILETTI
CON SPINACI
Cod 'Florentine'

Why is the term 'Florentine' associated with spinach? I have not been able to find out the answer. Larousse informs me that spinach is of Persian origin, unknown to the Romans and transplanted to Europe by the Moors. And no Italian recipes that I have discovered associate Florence with this splendid vegetable. The term seems to have been evolved by the French, so I suppose fish and eggs cooked in this way should strictly be classified as French dishes. When I think of doing this I am immediately confronted with a recurrence of *Sauce Mornay* (page 162) which I am anxious should not haunt – a substantial golden ghost – the pages of this book.

Can I solve this problem by altering my sauce to one of an Italian type? I think so, because I am determined to include a combination of fish and spinach.

Constance Spry in her magisterial style pronounces as follows:

'Before two wars had revolutionised our menus it was unusual for a green vegetable to be served with fish, unless perhaps green peas with salmon. Now that fish has so often to be a main course green vegetables are very commonly handed with it. I still dislike the combination of flavours, yet the following may be counted an exception. "Florentine" indicates the inclusion of spinach.'

She goes on to give the classic dish, including, of course, *Sauce Mornay*. Yet, before I give my own 'Italian' version, I pause to brood on her remarks about fish and green vegetables ('green' being the operative word). Do I agree with them? I find I do, with the exception of the courgette. (Of course, green herbs of innumerable kinds are essential to fish cookery.) But fish with cauliflower, with cabbage, with brussels sprouts – no, a thousand times. Even the thought of freshly cooked asparagus as an accompaniment leaves me uneasy.

1kg (2¼lb) fresh spinach

4 fillets cod, skinned (other non-oily
fish, such as turbot, halibut, John Dory,
plaice, fresh haddock will do)

150ml (¼ pint) *court-bouillon* (use the
one for Scallops with Mussels, page 50)

100g (4oz) butter

½ teaspoon salt

½ teaspoon freshly ground black pepper

2 eggs, lightly beaten

50g (2oz) finely grated Parmesan cheese

Wash the spinach well, cook it for 5 minutes in 600ml (1 pint)
water, drain it thoroughly and chop it finely. Now put the fish to
poach gently in the *court-bouillon*. Put the spinach in a saucepan
with the butter and seasonings and cook for 4 minutes, stirring
constantly. Turn off the flame but keep the pan on the stove. Mix
in the beaten eggs, add the cheese and cook, stirring constantly,
for 2–3 minutes. Lift the fillets from the *court-bouillon* on to a
previously heated serving dish. Pour the spinach-cheese mixture
over, and serve at once.

TONNO AL POMODORO
Tuna with Tomato Sauce

How difficult it is to find this splendid firm fish nowadays. I
suppose it has all gone to the 'canneries' for 'packing' in strange
and undesirable oils.

Tuna is a very popular fish in Italy. There is a long tradition there of preserving it at home in *olive* oil with bay leaves, peppercorns and salt. However, for this recipe, fresh tuna – or tunny, as I always used to call it – is essential.

Serves 4–6

900g (2lb) tuna, cut into steaks about 5cm (2in) thick, dipped in flour
4 tablespoons olive oil
1 small onion, sliced
2 cloves garlic, crushed
4 tablespoons tomato purée
300ml (½ pint) warm water
150ml (¼ pint) dry white wine
1 tablespoon parsley
¼ teaspoon salt
½ teaspoon freshly ground black pepper

Cook the tuna steaks for a few moments in the olive oil, until the flour is golden. Set them aside in a cooking pan in which you can serve them at table. Cook the onion and garlic in the olive oil until soft and transparent. Dissolve the tomato purée in the warm water, then add the wine and the other ingredients and bring to a boil in the pan with the olive oil, garlic and onions. Cook rapidly for about 1 minute. Now pour the mixture over the tuna and simmer gently for 10 minutes.

SOGLIOLE VERDI
Sole Verdi

This is our most opulent Italian main course. Or it could be the first course at a dinner party, if you follow it with something rather austere.

Serves 3–6

---

6 fillets sole, skinned, each weighing
150g (6oz)

100g (4oz) butter

300ml (½ pint) dry white wine

---

salt and pepper

---

1 teaspoon fresh basil leaves,
very finely chopped

---

1 tablespoon parsley, finely chopped

15g (½oz) flour

---

2 tablespoons single cream

50g (2oz) finely grated Parmesan cheese

Place the fillets side by side in a fireproof dish which has been rubbed over with 25g (1oz) butter. Pour the wine over them, then sprinkle on salt and pepper, 50g (2oz) melted butter and the basil and parsley. Cover the dish with foil and bake in a moderate oven (Gas 4/180°C/350°F) for 25 minutes. Take from the oven, and carefully remove the fillets from the dish. Pour the juices into a jug. Rearrange the fillets in the dish, and keep warm. Make a *roux* with the remaining butter and flour, and pour on the juices. Allow to thicken quickly, stirring constantly, and blending in the cream at the last moment. Pour the sauce over the fillets. Sprinkle with the grated Parmesan, and brown swiftly under a preheated grill.

O sogliole mio!

One is hot and one is cold . . .

SALSA ALLA PIZZAIOLA
Pizzaiola Sauce

This sauce, though its interpretation – as ever – varies slightly from cook to cook, is the basic sauce used in Naples for that city's beloved pizza. It is also used for grilled meat, pasta and . . . fish. Alan Davidson, in his *Mediterranean Seafood,* suggests it is ideal for fish which are past their prime or not especially interesting in flavour. I agree with him heartily, though my recipe is not the same as his. I winced the other day when I saw a recipe for smothering whole sole in this sauce, but when it comes to that rather tired bit of coley . . . Alas, I sound as if I am maligning the sauce, which I am not. It is excellent . . . vigorous and heartening.

2 cloves garlic, crushed
75ml (3 fl. oz) olive oil
675g (1½lb) ripe tomatoes, peeled and roughly chopped
3 anchovy fillets, pounded
½ teaspoon coarsely ground black pepper
for garnish
½ teaspoon fresh oregano leaves, chopped
1 teaspoon parsley, coarsely chopped

Cook the garlic in the oil. Add the tomatoes, anchovy fillets, and pepper. Cover over a high flame for about 15 minutes, until the sauce has reduced and merged, but is not smooth. Pour over your poached fillets or steaks of fish. Sprinkle with the oregano and parsley and serve.

Note: If you are not using fresh oregano, add the dried oregano at the same time as the tomatoes, etc.

PESTO
Basil Sauce

This is the cold one . . . far less respectable than the hot for *my* purposes. No one ever suggests serving *pesto* with fish. It is ordained that it should be eaten either with pasta or in minestrone because of its pungent flavour. Eating grilled steaks of the less scintillating fish, and when plates of – often hard-to-identify – 'small fry' are brought to the table at a lengthy *mezé,* how often I have yearned for a bowl of fragrant green-glowing *pesto.* (And if you are sometimes compelled to share a feast of fish-fingers with your children – how *pesto* would brighten your – grilled – share of the banquet!)

50–75g (2–3oz) fresh basil leaves, without stems
4 cloves garlic, peeled and crushed
5 tablespoons olive oil
4 level tablespoons pine-nut kernels
6 heaped tablespoons Parmesan cheese, very finely grated

Those who are fond of spending unnecessary (as opposed to vital) hours in their kitchens may go through the process of pounding this mixture with a pestle in a mortar. There are recipes which necessitate this (see *Tarama,* page 131) but *pesto* is not one of them. Anyone who can afford the ingredients for *pesto* can afford a modest blender. Put everything in – except the cheese, which would make the mixture sticky and difficult to handle. When all is smooth, remove to a bowl and carefully stir in the Parmesan. (Some like one-third Pecorino cheese, but not me.)

Notes: a It is said that a half-quantity of green dried basil, reconstituted with an equal amount of water that has been boiled and then cooled, will 'work' if you cannot obtain fresh basil. I haven't tried this, and the idea fills me with suspicion.

b I have preserved *pesto* in a jar in the refrigerator for two weeks by leaving a small space at the top which I filled with olive oil after the *pesto* had 'set'. I then screwed the lid on tightly. I have heard that *pesto* can be sealed with a thin layer of melted butter. Again . . . I haven't tried it.

It is obvious that one could write a thesis on *pesto,* but I shall say no more except, 'Beloved Genoa! When I last visited you, I was enraged by your traffic problems and astonished by your museum of Japanese pornography (I wonder if this still exists?). However when I think of you as the parent of *pesto,* you shoot to the top of my list of favourite Italian cities.'

Greece

I first encountered the soup which follows – *Kakavia* – on Aghios Nikolaos where an unwritten law gave the freedom of the island to the fishing crews from Khalia, the nearest village on the mainland, in which some twenty of the part-owners of the island lived. Francis Turville-Petre, who was trying to buy the island outright, had already persuaded these twenty part-owners to accept his offer for the freehold. Now he faced the task of persuading some further fifty part-owners who had emigrated to the United States.

It was all very irritating, and when the Khalia fishing-fleet of about fifteen stalwarts first arrived on the island to camp out and cook, make free with his resinated wine and dance and sing for most of the night, Francis had been as cross as two sticks at what he considered to be an infringement of his seigniory of the island. However, he soon became reconciled to the ancient tradition, and would indeed join in and encourage the festivity. These incursions took place perhaps once every two months, and the fishermen would cook their own food in tin-lined copper pots as big as buckets. Their main dish was the *kakavia* which has as many variations as the bouillabaisse, if not more. (Alan Davidson tells us in *Mediterranean Seafood* that 'There are Greeks who maintain that the bouillabaisse of Marseilles is of Greek origin, and that Greek fish soup is the fundamental and oldest one in the Mediterranean.') Any fish and any vegetable available are often flung into it – indiscriminately, in the case of the fishermen from Khalia. Another problem was that, in their state of Bacchic euphoria, those responsible for cooking the *kakavia* had lost all sense of time, and when I came to sample it, most of the fish, apart from fragments of squid and octopus, had turned into cotton wool through long-overboiling. *Kakavia* is normally served over slices of bread – an idea which I don't care for anyway – but the fisher-chefs had cast this into the soup while it cooked. Crusts floated on the surface, together with some onion skins, a few fish-heads, and a couple of sucked-looking lemon halves. However, when I managed to extract some of the broth, highly scented with garlic and rosemary, I found it delicious.

I can't really attempt to reproduce that soup in a recipe. What follows, though tidier, has undoubtedly lost some of the original fine careless rapture.

KAKAVIA
Greek Fish Soup

Serves up to 12

7 large tomatoes, skinned and chopped

6 onions, coarsely chopped

4 cloves garlic, crushed

150ml (¼ pint) olive oil

300ml (½ pint) white resinated wine

2 sticks celery

2 tablespoons fennel root,
finely chopped

2 bay leaves

1 tablespoon thyme, finely chopped

1 tablespoon parsley, finely chopped

2 sprigs rosemary

2 carrots, finely chopped

1 teaspoon salt

2 teaspoons ground black pepper

1.75 litres (3 pints) water

juice of 2 lemons

1kg (2¼lb) conger eel

6 rascasses *or* 3 small gurnard, cleaned

6 small red mullet

Put all the above ingredients, except the fish, in a large pot, bring to the boil and allow to simmer for 1 hour. By then there will have been a general melding together. Now chop your conger eel into large segments, put them into the soup and cook for 15 minutes. Test the conger eel to see if it is almost cooked. If so, add the rascasses (or gurnard) and the mullet and gently simmer for a further 15 minutes.

Distribute the fish on soup plates – over slices of bread or toast, if you must, but I would strongly discourage it – and ladle on sufficient of the broth and its contents to cover the fish.

TARAMA
Fish-roe Spread

I am so tired of *taramasalata,* more often than not an insipid pink mixture which lacks the essential taste of preserved roe. I have always preferred *tarama,* which you could define as either a 'pâté'* or a 'spread'. Oh, that it could be made with *avgotarakho* (the dried, pressed, smoked eggs of the grey mullet). But this, even when I was in Athens in 1934, was very expensive: a *mezé* you had to *pay for* outside Orphanides' Bar (*mezés* were free when you bought a drink, in those days), and it came in thin, thin slivers. Nowadays it *can* be obtained in Athens but costs almost as much as caviare. However, if you are a millionaire, use it as the basis of this invigorating paste. Otherwise . . . make do with smoked cod's roe.

---

*As has been pointed out by Elizabeth David, the term 'pâté' applied to fish is incorrect; the term used should be ¡paste'. But we shall have a hard time persuading *restaurateurs* and hostesses to accept this.

131

100g (4oz) *avgotarakho or* 225g (8oz) smoked cod's roe
juice of 1 or 2 lemons
black pepper
150ml (¼ pint) virgin olive oil

If you are using smoked cod's roe, scoop it from its skin. Put it or the *avgotarakho* into a mortar (not the blender, for this) and pound it very slowly with the lemon juice and black pepper. Drip in the olive oil, and pound till you have a thick smooth paste. Serve very cold with pitta bread or hot toast.

PSARI PLAKI
Greek Fish

As its title suggests, this recipe features the Greek national way with fish. It has many variations and no one recipe for it will be exactly the same as any other. Ingredients used, which I have not included, are spinach, dill, mint, olives, *rigani* (the Greek variety of oregano), bay leaves, breadcrumbs and, very often, lemon juice which I, and many Greek cooks, believe is here in conflict with the white wine (some, of course, omit the wine). Sometimes it is served hot and sometimes cold, and often (in Greek fashion) lukewarm. It can be cooked over a flame (as it often was in the old days when many people did not possess ovens) or baked in the oven. You can make it with any firm white fish: sometimes several smaller ones, occasionally a whole large one, but most often – as here – with a large fish cut into steaks or slices. The 'constants' seem to be tomatoes, onions and olive oil. (I would have added garlic, but restrained myself in view of today's garlic-shunning – shades of Dracula! – Mediterranean bourgeoisie.) Also it is always laid out flat, usually in a shallow pan. (The Greek word *plakotos* means 'flat'.)

As you will have gathered, I can make no claim for the version I give here to be, in any sense, authoritative.

Serves 6

---

3 onions, chopped

---

2 carrots, sliced

---

1 stick celery, sliced

---

2 cloves garlic, crushed

1kg (2¼lb) large white fish (grouper,
sea–bream, sea–bass, cod), cut into steaks

---

6 tablespoons olive oil

---

6 tomatoes, skinned and coarsely
chopped

---

1 glass white wine

---

salt and black pepper

---

for garnish

---

2 tablespoons parsley, chopped

Fry together, till tender, the onions, carrots, celery and garlic in 3 tablespoons of the oil. Lay the fish steaks in a shallow baking dish, brushed with oil. Pour over the fried vegetables and cover with the tomatoes. Now pour on the wine, and sprinkle with the remaining oil, adding salt and pepper. Bake for 30 minutes at Gas 5/190°C/375°F. Sprinkle with the chopped parsley, and serve immediately.

ATHENAIKI
MAYONAISA
Athens Fish Mayonnaise

I ate this dish recently in a private house, on a very hot day, and it was extremely pleasant. It is easy to make, if you have a large mould shaped like a fish. My Greek hostess evidently possessed one, for the great cream-coloured creature at the centre of the serving table had clearly marked, though rather sombre, features, and fins, scales and a tail. His eyes were slices of cucumber with pimento pupils, and a line of cucumber slices ran down his spine. He rested on a lavish bed of parsley.

I accepted my portion of his flesh, and at once recognised its freshness and the excellence of the light, lemony mayonnaise which permeated it. I asked my hostess for her recipe, which was very simple. (I am afraid, in this case, it is impossible to provide quantities.)

The day before, she had obtained from a fisherman two fresh-caught, very large grey mullet, which she immediately cleaned and poached in a *court-bouillon*. When the fish were cooked and had cooled, she carefully skinned them and removed their bones. She then broke their flesh into small pieces and combined these with enough home-made mayonnaise (the quantity must have been vast) for the mixture to become homogeneous and easily pressed into the mould. This was at once put in the refrigerator. Thence, today, the fish had emerged only an hour before lunch, to be 'turned out' in its new identity (a mystic marriage: two mullet had become one), given eyes, garnished, and – reclining on its parsley bed – replaced in the refrigerator until the guests were summoned to the feast.

How delightful – and how hygienic, too. So perhaps you will wonder why, at first sight of the huge fish, I had to restrain myself from physically recoiling in fear. The reason was that I had met so many of his poor relations, who in many cases were not only poor but dangerous.

All over the Greek-speaking world, the *Athenaiki Mayonaisa* has proliferated, and especially among *restaurateurs*. In many hotels it has become the centrepiece of the obligatory twice-weekly buffet and is presented with the pomp with which, in vanished days, a spun-sugar château, fortress or cathedral was proudly wheeled into the dining-room – for display purposes only – by the ship's chef on the last night of an ocean voyage.

It must be difficult to make a spun-sugar cathedral, and – even when his masterpiece had, over the years, become somewhat shabby – I always thought the ship's chef's pride was justified. I cannot say the same about most perpetrators of the Athens Fish Mayonnaise concoction: an exact description, for invariably they have eked out the fish-content with such economical inclusions as so-called 'Russian' salad, boiled potatoes, tinned peas and pickled gherkins, while the mayonnaise is undoubtedly delivered at the service entrance in vats from the local 'industrial estate'.

Even with regard to that original innocent and charming fish, I have doubts, though of another kind. While I am fond of mayonnaise as a sauce or coating, I do not like it to form an adhesive, holding food together, or to play an equal (even dominant) rôle, to that of the main ingredient in a dish.

KALAMARI SALATA
Squid Salad

With what relief I turn to this honest and savoury dish. It is my idea of a satisfactory summer meal.

Serves 6

675g (1½lb) tiny squid
6 tablespoons olive oil
3 cloves garlic, crushed
1 bay leaf
3 tablespoons red wine

3 tablespoons water	
a generous pinch of salt	
2 tablespoons lemon juice	
black pepper from a mill	
for garnish	
1 tablespoon parsley	

This must be made with really tiny squid which, after cleaning and removal of the ink-sacs, can be cut longitudinally, into fine strips instead of the familiar rings.

Sauté the squid very gently in the olive oil, with the garlic, for about 8 minutes. Then add the bay leaf, red wine, water and salt. Stew on a very low heat until the squid is tender (about 30 minutes). Allow to cool, then arrange on a dish. Sprinkle with the lemon juice. Grind on some black pepper and scatter with parsley. Chill before serving.

HELI YAHNISTO
Eel Stew

This is another honest and simple dish, eaten by people on the coast in winter.

I have always thought that its simplicity was one of the great merits of Greek cooking, so you can imagine my surprise when I learnt recently from a highly tendentious 'cookery book' published in Athens that the world's most sophisticated cuisines were all Greek in origin. Until they first came in contact with the Greeks, the poor Romans' 'sole dish' (I quote) was 'a type of gruel'. As for the Turks, regard for international relations forbids me to say more. And I was very grieved to learn that nineteen listed 'authors of the culinary arts' (one of whom 'wrote eleven books on "SUPPERS DESCRIPTIONS"') were 'all unlucky' because their entire works were lost in the fire which destroyed the Library of Alexandria during the seventh century AD.

Anyway, I am simple enough to enjoy this eel stew. And if any of you are 'afraid' of eels, please let me reassure you. Your fishmonger will skin them and remove their heads. He will even cut them into slices for you. The contents of your parcel will be in no way reminiscent of the living creature. In addition, which is important, eels are delicious.

Serves 6

1kg (2¼lb) skinned eel, cut into 5–7cm (2–3in) slices

---

3 tablespoons olive oil

---

2 medium sized onions, chopped

---

2 cloves garlic, crushed

150ml (¼ pint) red wine

---

1 dessertspoon red wine vinegar

---

1 sprig rosemary

---

2 bay leaves

1½ tablespoons parsley, coarsely chopped

---

salt and black pepper

Heat the olive oil in a small flameproof casserole. Put in the onions and garlic to cook until soft. Add the red wine, wine vinegar and herbs, and heat to boiling point, when you should reduce heat immediately. Now put in your slices of eel. Allow all to cook gently on top of the stove at a low heat for 25 minutes. Season to taste, and serve with good crusty bread.

PSARIA MARINATA
Island Marinated Fish

This recipe is taken from Theonie Mark's *Greek Island Cooking*. I have included it here for two reasons. The first is that I tried it and found it good; the second is that it made me think of all those isolated parts of the British Isles where the friendly fishmonger is never seen, and the only fish within shopping distance is crumbed and frozen or tinned in unpleasant oil. Why shouldn't wistful fish-lovers in such regions, after their occasional trips to the nearest city, make up large quantities of this nice recipe? 'Weekend commuters', also, could keep crocks of it in the larders of their country cottages.

'In the past, the few times that fresh fish was available during the winter in the islands, people bought it in big quantities, which they cooked and preserved in a strong marinade sauce so that they could keep the fish a long time and use it up slowly. This method has been in use since ancient times and is still in use today in villages where refrigeration is not available. In the cities, however, fish is marinated this way today primarily because people like it so much. Small fish like large smelts and whitebait are used, cleaned and left whole.

Serves 5

3 pounds smelts or whitebait

salt and pepper to taste

flour for rolling plus 3 tablespoons

olive oil for frying
3 cloves finely minced garlic
1 cup hot water
½ cup white or red wine vinegar
1 teaspoon dried rosemary

'Clean, gut and degill the fish, leaving the heads on; then rinse them under running cold water, season them with salt and pepper, and let them stand at room temperature for 10 minutes. Then dip them in flour and tap them to shake off the excess. Put enough olive oil in a skillet to cover the bottom at least ¼ inch deep, heat it over moderate heat until a haze forms, and fry the fish a few at a time until they are golden on both sides. Remove them to a deep clay or earthenware bowl and keep them warm. Strain the remaining oil from the skillet into a saucepan and over moderate heat sauté the garlic until it is light golden. Add 3 tablespoons of flour and stir constantly until the flour is absorbed by the oil, then slowly add 1 cup of hot water and bring it to a boil. Continuing to stir, add the vinegar and rosemary and season with salt and pepper to taste. Simmer the sauce uncovered for 5 minutes. Pour the sauce over the fish in the earthenware bowl and serve hot or cold.'

Note: Mrs Mark is not referring to our English whitebait, unknown on the Greek islands or in the United States, where she now lives. (If one were to 'clean, gut and degill' them, they would cease to exist.) The fish she refers to are what we would call 'sprats'.

Two sauces

I conclude with two (*the* two?) classic Greek sauces: poles apart, but each, in its own way, delicious with fish. One is the gentle *Avgolemono,* the other the pungent *Skordalia.*

SALSA AVGOLEMONO
Egg and Lemon Sauce

This is a very adaptable sauce, for, according to what dish you intend it to accompany, you choose the stock to make it with: lamb, chicken, or, in this case, fish. *Avgolemono Psarasoupa,* for which a recipe is given on page 176, derives from it.

2 egg yolks
juice of 1 good-sized lemon
300ml (½ pint) fish stock (see page 113)
salt

Beat the egg yolks with the lemon juice. Then heat the stock to boiling point and let it stand to cool for 3 minutes. Now pour a ladle of stock on to the egg and lemon, whisking all well together. Add the rest of the stock very gradually, beating with your whisk all the time till it thickens. Season with salt to taste. The sauce can be reheated but you must never let it boil, or the egg will curdle.

I particularly enjoy this sauce when it is poured over poached fish, and then sprinkled with parsley. It can also be served cold – an ethereal cousin of the sturdy mayonnaise. Whether it is hot or cold, herbs can be incorporated in it just before serving – for instance, parsley, dill or tarragon, finely chopped.

SKORDALIA
Garlic Sauce

Those whose love-objects or business associates are averse to the magic bulb should definitely shun this uncooked garlic sauce. Usually it is eaten with fried fish, but I enjoy it with grilled steaks, of such fish as halibut, fresh haddock, hake. Do not choose a fish of very delicate and subtle flavour.

8 slices day-old white bread, with crusts removed
8 cloves garlic, peeled and chopped
salt
150ml (¼ pint) olive oil
3 tablespoons white wine vinegar

Soak the bread in a small quantity of water for several minutes. Meanwhile, pound the garlic, with a little salt, in a mortar. (This is one of those cases where the blender just won't do.) Now squeeze the water out of the bread with your hands, kneading it until soft and smooth. Next, pound it with the garlic until they are amalgamated. Gradually add the olive oil, first drop by drop, then in a thin stream, continuing to pound all the time until the oil is absorbed. Finally, stir in the wine vinegar.

Many variants of this sauce are possible. To start with, I am sure that many people will say I have used too much garlic. (Some, more refined, authors recommend only three cloves.) There are those who incorporate crushed almonds or walnuts into the sauce. Others use potatoes instead of bread, or combine the two. A grander, more *aïoli*-like version can be produced by adding the yolk of an egg. Chopped parsley may be stirred in. But none of these variations are for me. On only one point am I neutral. If you want to, substitute lemon juice for wine vinegar. (In this case, use 2 tablespoons instead of 3.) As I noted earlier, it is the honesty and simplicity of most Greek cookery that appeals to me, and I like *skordalia* chaste and unadorned.

South Africa

My wife spent eleven turbulent years in South Africa. My own experience was briefer. In 1941, *en route* for the Middle East, I was on a troopship which docked for three days in Cape Town.

'Oh,' said my wife when I first mentioned this to her, 'did you go to the Harbour Café?' And she proceeded to talk of oysters and also of giant 'crayfish' (as South Africans call crawfish), grilled and brushed with melted butter.

At the time of my visit to Cape Town, I was an acting unpaid lance corporal in the Military Police, and – feeling rather like the hounds of spring on winter's traces – I spent my stay in pursuit of an interesting band of immature soldiers.

There was the young classical scholar for whom the public lavatories of the port had an appeal so strong that it attracted the unfriendly attention of the local police. There was the poet who, on our first day in port, fell in love with a South African girl and vowed that he would never, never leave her. (I had to drag him back to the ship by force.) There was the Rural Dean's son who managed to get lost during a solitary stroll on the lower slopes of Table Mountain. Finally – and he eluded me entirely – there was the detected murderer, captive on the ship, who escaped and was never seen again. No, alas, I had not visited the Harbour Café.

'Sad!' said my wife, and we went on to discuss South African fish cookery. Raw oysters, grilled crustacea and smoked snoek were the things that lingered in her memory. '*Snoek?*' I queried, remembering an extraordinary substance in a tin which, together with whalemeat steaks, struck terror into British hearts in the immediate post-war period. However, freshly caught and then smoked, snoek is apparently extraordinary in quite a different sense.

Of more complicated fish cuisine (apart from how she herself had baked a fine scarlet fish called a Red Roman with herbs and wine), my wife had little to report. However, there was one South African fish dish of which she approved highly. And, of course, my visit to Cape Town is merely the pretext for including in this book a recipe for –

INGELEGTE VIS
Pickled Fish

In the event, my wife has presented me with *three* recipes!

The first is taken from *Cape Cookery*, published in Cape Town in 1890.

'For this, *geelbeck* is the best. Cut the fish into slices about one inch in thickness. Sprinkle them with salt and pepper and put them aside till next day; put them out in the air till they are rather dry. Have some onions sliced, cut chillies, bay leaves, turmeric and vinegar, all in proportion to the fish; boil all up. The onions must not be too much cooked. Put the fish into a deep earthenware jar, in layers with onions between each layer. Pour over the vinegar and cover closely. In two days it will be fit to use but will keep for a long time.'

This has the charming vagueness (charming to the casual reader; nightmarish to the cook) of many old recipes, and I would not recommend your following it. The next recipe, which is from the *Victory Cookbook*, published in Cape Town in the early 1940s, in aid of war charities, is far more practicable. This features the Cape way of preserving fish.

Ingredients:

2 good-sized soles, *or* any nice Cape fish, filleted [about 2¼lb firm white fish]
6 large onions
2oz [50g] curry powder
1oz [25g] Mango Relish [this means mango chutney]
6 large or 12 small chillies
1 quart vinegar
salt to taste

'Fry the fish a nice brown in lard, butter or olive oil; drain and cool. Slice 4 onions and fry a nice brown in a little oil; add 1oz curry powder, 2 chillies, cut fine, a dessertspoon salt, and the Mango Relish. When stirred to a paste, add a little vinegar to moisten well; then lay the fish in a jar; spread over each layer some of this mixture. Cut the rest of the onions in rings; boil in the vinegar very gently, until quite tender, with the other ounce of curry powder and a little salt; then pour over the fish. Let it stand to cool, then cork well. It will be fit for use in two or three days, and will keep for months. It is a delicious breakfast or lunch dish.'

Notes: **a** I would recommend olive oil rather than lard or butter.

b The author has forgotten the rest of the chillies. I feel sure that these (cut fine like the others) should be boiled with the onions, etc.

c The old wide-topped earthenware jars used for preserving (we have some in Cyprus) had big round flat corks; hence the reference to corking, which may puzzle some modern readers. Nowadays, if preserving in an earthenware jar, I would advise sealing very carefully with foil; otherwise use a glass preserving jar, with the lid tightly closed.

d Oh, for an appetite from the wide-open spaces, so that I could consume this dish for *breakfast*!

My wife has followed this recipe and confirms that it is satisfactory. However, a moody look appeared on her face. 'The best pickled fish I ever ate,' she said, 'was at Len Bloom's flat in Cape Town. I wish we had his recipe.'

Our friend, Leonard Bloom, now lives in London where we have eaten many delicious meals cooked by him. We got in touch with him to ask for his recipe. After reading it, my wife said, '*Was this what I ate in Cape Town? It sounds wildly exotic. Anyway, it is sure to be wonderful.'*

We have christened this recipe (reproduced here in Len Bloom's own words)

BLOOM'S BAROQUE
PICKLED FISH

1kg (2¼lb) thick cutlets or fillets of any
firm white fish: eg, cod or carp (if you
should be so lucky as to find some)

matzo meal for coating

6 large onions

oil for frying

25g (1oz) turmeric

15g (½oz) ground ginger
or finely sliced fresh ginger

1 teaspoon ground coriander

as much cumin as you can stomach

1 teaspoon mustard powder

50g (2oz) – say, 2 hefty dessertspoons –
of sweet mango chutney (particularly
agreeable is Sharwood's Mango and
Ginger Chutney)

1 teaspoon chilli powder *or* 2 or 3 small
hot chillies, chopped

1.25 litres (2 pints) white wine vinegar
or, if you can get it, Dufrais Bistro Chef
(white wine + grape juice +
wine vinegar)

salt

'Coat the fish in fine matzo meal. Fry it, and leave to cool on greaseproof paper. Slice the onions finely and fry until soft – not brown – in oil. Then add in the dry ingredients and chutney, and thin with the vinegar, mixing vigorously. Bring to the boil and allow to stand while you arrange the first layer of fish in a dish that can be covered closely.

'Cover the fish in the vinegar mixture. Then lay down another layer of fish. Cover in vinegar, and so on. Make sure that all the vinegar is used up.

'Cover the dish closely, keep cold, and leave for as long as you can resist temptation.'

Notes: a 'as much cumin as you can stomach'; I would say 1 teaspoonful.
       b If you are going to keep the fish for a long time, I would suggest white wine vinegar as opposed to Bistro Chef. (I think I might in any case.)

The third recipe is definitely my favourite. Both it and the previous one should serve six to ten people.

Turkey and Lebanon

Imagine my astonishment and delight at finding in Arto der Haroutunian's *Middle Eastern Cookery* what was surely that same dish of stuffed mussels from which I had been so rudely dragged by that air-raid warning in Istanbul during the war. Yes, it was the very same, for Mr der Haroutunian attributes it to Tokatlian at whose hotel I was eating it.

MIDYA LITSK
Stuffed Mussels Served Cold

Serves 4–6 people

about 30 mussels

4–6 tablespoons olive oil

2 medium onions, finely chopped

75g (3oz) rice, washed thoroughly

50g (2oz) pine-nut kernels or walnuts,
coarsely chopped

50g (2oz) currants

1 tablespoon parsley, chopped

1 heaped teaspoon salt

1 level teaspoon allspice

½ teaspoon chilli pepper

for garnish

lemon wedges

'Put the mussels to soak in a large saucepan filled with salted water. Discard any mussels with open or broken shells or any that float to the surface.

'To prepare the filling, first heat 4–6 tablespoons of olive oil in a saucepan, add the onions and fry until soft. Add the rice and fry for about 3–5 minutes, stirring frequently to prevent sticking. Stir in all the remaining ingredients and cook for a further 5–10 minutes. Taste and adjust seasoning if necessary. Remove from the heat.

'Scrub and wash each musselshell thoroughly. Force open each mussel with a sharp knife. If you find them difficult to open put them in a very thick-bottomed saucepan, cover, put over a low heat and steam for a few minutes – they should then begin to open. Cut off the beard – the fibrous bits that keep the mussel attached to its shell – but do not remove the flesh. Leave in slightly salted water until ready to use.

'To fill, take one mussel at a time and put a teaspoon of the filling inside – do not pack too tightly as the rice will swell when cooked. If you loosen the joint a little the shell should stay closed, but if not tie up with cotton. Pack tightly into a saucepan, cover with an inverted plate to stop the mussels moving while cooking, and pour in enough water to cover. Bring to the boil then lower the heat and simmer for 1–1½ hours. Drain off the water, allow to cool and arrange on a serving dish with lemon wedges.'

Note: Thanks to the advances of modern science, you can, instead of tying up each mussel with cotton to hold it together, wrap it in a small piece of silver foil.

On my first arrival in Turkey, very early in 1944, I was for a short season quite popular with my colleagues. As I was a newcomer, many tedious chores could be dumped on me, such as the weekly or monthly summaries, audit boards to check up on the Assistant Military Attaché's accounts, and other such matters for which I had little qualification. Socially I was thought to lend a certain cachet to supper or drinking parties by my exceptional talent for balancing an open bottle of champagne on my head, lowering myself slowly to the ground, stretching out on my stomach for a short period of display, and then slowly gathering myself up into a crouching position and rising gradually therefrom to my feet, the bottle still balanced on my head, not a drop being spilt. I would then distribute its contents to an admiring throng of cypher girls and their escorts.

It was not possible for me to display this special talent of mine in restaurants like Tokatlian's, Abdullah's or the Buyukdere taverna. I reserved it for private houses, except when occasionally – replacing the champagne with a bottle of rough red wine – I would feel sufficiently uplifted to repeat this performance, which involved my first going almost into a state of trance, in humble waterside eating-places where we would be likely to be served a simple menu such as the one which now follows.

FISH KEBAB

The kebab is probably the most famous form of Middle Eastern cookery, and the one I came upon most often in Turkey. Fish are excellent cooked in this way, provided they are properly marinated and not *over*-cooked. Swordfish is the most usual fish to be cooked on a skewer but, if you cannot obtain it, halibut or any other firm white fish can be used. Kebabs are best cooked over charcoal, of course, but can be cooked under the grill of an ordinary stove.

Serves 4–6

1kg (2¼lb) firm white fish, filleted

for the marinade

4 cloves garlic, crushed

2 anchovy fillets, pounded

300ml (½ pint) water

300ml (½ pint) white wine

3 tablespoons white wine vinegar

juice of 1 lemon

2 bay leaves

1 dessertspoon parsley, finely chopped

1 dessertspoon thyme, finely chopped

Cut the fish into what Americans would call 'bite-size' cubes, and lay them in the marinade, with all the ingredients well mixed, for at least 2 hours before you skewer them. You can put rings of onion or sweet peppers between the cubes of fish on the skewer, but this is not customary (though soaked bay leaves are sometimes used in this way). Baste the cubes with the marinade, turning frequently till they are brown on the outside but not too soft within (about 10 minutes).

Pilaffs

There are two classic Turkish accompaniments to fish kebabs: a pilaff and Tarator Sauce.

I give here a recipe for a very simple pilaff. All the same, you will notice that the rice is not 'plain boiled' but fried: in butter, or *ghee* or often, in Egypt, oil, before water is added to it. It is interesting that people from hot countries have, on the whole, an aversion to 'boiling'. It is the same in India. I remember, in Ruth Prawer Jhabvala's novel *Esmond in India,* how all the Indian relatives of the half-Indian, half-English child were deeply shocked when his English father insisted on his eating *boiled food.* As far as I am concerned, English cooking, in its darkest days, heavily depended on boiling as a cookery method. Boiling – as opposed to poaching – fish has always been anathema to me (and, oh, those awful vegetables, boiled to death: especially the cabbage which, cooked for 2–3 minutes, as I do it, does not exude that abominable boarding-house smell!).

SIMPLE PILAFF

225g (8oz) long-grain rice

50g (2oz) butter, *ghee or* oil (as this recipe is Turkish not Egyptian, I would recommend butter or *ghee* – clarified butter. See page 167.)

1 teaspoon salt

600ml (1 pint) boiling water

Bring the water to the boil. Melt the butter or *ghee* in a saucepan and add the rice, allowing it to fry for 3 minutes or so, until translucent. Add the boiling water and the salt. Allow to boil for 2 minutes. Now cover the pan and let the rice simmer very gently until all the liquid has been absorbed. Turn off the heat, cover the rice with kitchen paper or a cloth, and put in the bottom of the oven at the lowest possible heat for about 10 minutes. It will be fluffy and ready to serve when you fork it through.

TARATOR SAUCE

This Turkish version of the sauce which I ate in Istanbul uses walnuts, instead of pine kernels as in other parts of the Middle East. It is excellent with charcoal-grilled fish.

the crumbs of 3 thick slices white bread
100g (4oz) shelled walnuts
6 cloves garlic, crushed★
6 tablespoons olive oil
1 teaspoon salt
juice of 3 lemons

Soak the breadcrumbs in a little water and squeeze with the hands to get rid of excess liquid (as with *Skordalia*, page 141). Pound the walnuts and then, in a food processor, blend with the bread-crumbs, garlic, olive oil, salt and lemon juice to a smooth paste.

After the simple pilaff which I have just given as an accompaniment to fish kebabs, I cannot resist producing a more opulent one. This is a fisherfolk recipe. It makes brilliant use of the fresh anchovy, beloved of the Turks and now often available in Britain.

★You *could* use only 3 cloves of garlic.

HAMSI TAVASI
Fresh Anchovies with Rice

Serves 4–6

1kg (2¼lb) fresh anchovies

salt (say, 4–6 tablespoons)

3 small onions, chopped

100g (4oz) butter

400g (14oz) long-grain clean rice

900ml (1½ pints) boiling water

1½ teaspoons sugar

1 tablespoon sultanas

3 tablespoons freshly cracked walnuts, ground

1 teaspoon allspice

1 teaspoon cinnamon

1 teaspoon salt

1½ teaspoons red pepper

1½ teaspoons black pepper

Lay the cleaned and de-boned anchovies in a large wide pan. Cover them generously with salt so that each individual fish is well powdered inside and out. (This preliminary salting – like a first stage on the route to preserving – gives the anchovies in this dish their special taste.) Cover, and leave in a cool place for at least 1 hour.

Fry the onions gently in the butter until soft. Add the rice, and fry for a further 6 minutes, stirring frequently. Now pour the boiling water on to the rice, and add the sugar, sultanas, walnuts, and all the seasonings. Let these cook together for about 3 minutes. Reduce heat to a minimum. Cover the pan, and allow to simmer gently until the rice has absorbed all the liquid.

Butter a large casserole. Now wash the anchovies free of all the salt which has been covering them (I repeat, for at least 1 hour). Spread half of them on the bottom of the buttered casserole. Pour over the rice and its accompaniments, and lay the rest of the anchovies on top. Cover, and cook in a moderately hot oven (Gas 5/190°C/375°F) for about 20 minutes. Serve with any seasonable salad.

In Lebanese cooking, fishermen's dishes feature strongly. I give here two versions of a particular favourite.

SAYYADIEH
Fisherman's Fish with Rice

First version

Serves 6

4 tablespoons olive oil

3 medium onions, finely chopped

900ml (1½ pints) water

1 teaspoon salt

1 teaspoon ground cumin

1kg (2¼lb) fillets cod, coley, haddock, hake or other non-oily fish

450g (1lb) long-grain rice

50g (2oz) pine-nut kernels

juice of 1 lemon

Heat 3 tablespoons of the oil in a large saucepan, and fry the onions until brown. Add the water, salt, and ground cumin. Simmer until the onions have almost melted. Add the fish and cook gently for 10 minutes. Remove fish and keep warm. Now take from the stock in which the fish has been cooked sufficient to cook the rice, in a separate pan, until tender and the stock absorbed. Spoon the rice into a shallow dish and lay the fish pieces on top. Gently fry the pine-nut kernels in the remaining tablespoon of oil until tender, and scatter them over the fish. Meanwhile, simmer and reduce the remaining stock, adding the juice of a lemon. Pour this over the fish and rice or serve it separately in a small jug.

Second version

4 whole non-oily white fish, such as cod, whiting, turbot, sole, each about 225g (8oz)
salt and black pepper
3 cloves garlic, finely chopped
1 teaspoon ground cumin
6 tablespoons olive oil
2 medium-sized onions, finely chopped
400g (14oz) long-grain rice
300–450ml (½–¾ pint) hot water
flour (for coating fish)
for garnish
lemon wedges and parsley sprigs

Scale and gut the fish, leaving the heads on (or get your friendly fishmonger to do this). Rinse, wipe dry and rub all surfaces with salt and pepper. Then set aside in a cool place for 45 minutes.

Blend the garlic and the cumin.

Using 3 tablespoons of the oil, in a deep pan, fry the onions gently for 15–20 minutes until very soft and golden brown. Now wash the rice, drain it and add it to the onions in the pan. Stir over medium heat for 2–3 minutes. Add the hot water, bring to the boil, cover and cook gently for 20 minutes.

Make 3 deep slits in both sides of the fish. Fill these slits with the blended garlic and cumin. Now roll the fish in flour and, using the remaining olive oil, shallow-fry the fish until nicely browned. Remove the fish to a dish and keep hot.

Spoon two tablespoons of the oil in which the fish was fried over the rice, which should have absorbed the water in which it was boiled. Stir carefully with a fork, cover the pan and let stand for 5 minutes.

Pile the rice on a platter, arrange the fish on top. Garnish with lemon wedges and parsley sprigs.

The Big Fish

Small fish, grilled or fried, and dishes of fish with rice, like the two just given, are for everyday fish-eating. But a whole big fish cooked in the oven has a celebratory 'special occasion' quality. Two recipes of this kind follow.

SAMAK BI TAHINA
Fish with Tahina

Serves 4–6

Nothing could be more redolent of the Middle East than *tahina,* a nut-tasting paste made from sesame seeds, toasted and crushed. (It is available from numerous Cypriot and other provision stores in Britain. It tends to separate in the jar, so always stir before using.)

In this recipe the fish is baked with the *tahina,* which is more usually served as a separate sauce (for example Tarator Sauce, page 151).

1 large fish (grouper would probably be used locally, but sea-bass or bream are good substitutes) weighing about 1kg (2¼lb)
1½ teaspoons salt
4 tablespoons olive oil
2 medium-sized onions, finely chopped
juice of a large lemon
4 tablespoons water
6 tablespoons *tahina*

Clean the fish and rub it all over with the salt. Refrigerate for several hours. When it is time to start cooking, bring out the fish and allow it to reach room temperature. Brush it with olive oil, inside and out, and bake in a preheated oven (Gas 5/190°C/375°F) for 20 minutes. Now carefully skin the fish. Fry the onions in olive oil until they take colour. Beat the lemon juice and water into the *tahina* until it is creamy. Now add the fried onions. Cover the skinned fish with this sauce, and bake in the oven for a further 15 minutes.

SAMAK HARRA
Hot Fish

This 'Big Fish' dish, contributed by Miss Soraya Antonius from her splendid *Simple Arab Cookery,* is a fitting and spectacular climax to any selection of dishes from the Middle East.

---

1 large fish of about 1½kg (3½lb) of the grouper type, but sea-bass or bream could – as in the previous recipe – be substituted

---

8 tablespoons olive oil

---

juice of ¼ lemon

---

1 dessertspoon sea salt

100g (4oz) shelled walnuts

---

1 large head garlic, divided into cloves and peeled

---

1 heaped teaspoon cayenne pepper

---

1 bunch green coriander (obtainable from Indian shops as 'fresh *dhania*')

---

for garnish

50g (2oz) pine-nut kernels, toasted (double this quantity – if you can afford it. Miss Antonius says, 'The more the better'!)

---

lemon slices

With a little of the oil and the juice of ¼ of a lemon, beaten together, brush the whole fish outside and inside. (Your fish will of course have been cleaned.)

Put 2 tablespoons of oil in a large pan in the oven to get hot at Gas 5/190°C/375°F. Then lay the whole fish in the pan. Cover with silver foil and bake for 30 minutes. While the fish is cooking, pound 4 tablespoons of oil together with the sea salt, the walnuts and the garlic. Bring to a smooth paste (you could use a food processor for this). Into a small pan, put 2 tablespoons of oil. When this is hot, add the paste and stir continuously while it sautés for 2 minutes. Then add the cayenne pepper.

When the paste is sizzling add the finely chopped green coriander, and stir while you cook for just under a minute. (The green coriander must on no account be allowed to burn and blacken.) Remove the mixture from the heat and quickly stir in the juice of 2 lemons. Now remove your fish from the oven and skin it, except for the head and tail which should remain 'au naturel'. Anoint the bright white fish with the paste mixture, plastering it on inside and out. If your coriander has not burned and turned black, the colour scheme will be impressive. Decorate with patterns of lemon slices and toasted pine-nut kernels. Serve at once with triangles of hot Arab bread, or with boiled potatoes.

France

My travels in France have not been extensive, and have taken place chiefly since the war. They are associated in my mind with, in one case, a virulent attack of tonsilitis which led to my having to have my tonsils removed at a hospital in Nice where, owing to negligent nursing, I almost bled to death and had to undergo vigorous cautery without an anaesthetic in order to stem the outflow of blood. A long convalescence in Menton followed, which gave me considerable opportunities for probing the cuisine of the Côte d'Azur and Provence. Another occasion is associated with my third honeymoon, a motoring odyssey in a tiny Hillman Minx down through the French Burgundy district to Venice. The journey through the Côte d'Or was made notable by a weekend sojourn in a château where, apart from the castle mosquitoes which were as big as butterflies (how I longed for my Cairo flit-gun), the enormous bedroom where we spent two nights was decorated, in all convenient corners and under the bed, with giant black bats hanging, as it were at attention, upside down.

Yet despite the fact that journeys in France have not been numerous, how can I possibly omit the rôle of this astonishing country in my enjoyment of eating and cooking? At the sight of that great ornamented structure, a Versailles of the palate: French cuisine, how can I fail to make an obeisance?

Ever since Catherine de Medici brought chefs (and forks) from Florence to Paris, France has adopted cookery with a fanatic and yet scrupulous passion. Episodes from French cuisinological history drift through my mind. I think of Durand, famous chef to the nobility, who reprimanded Marie Antoinette for putting the mustard in a salad dressing before the salt, and after the Revolution started the world's first restaurant. I think of the Prince de Condé's chef, Vatel, who committed suicide when the fish he had ordered for a dinner arrived too late. I think of the rage for turkey stuffed with truffles which brought many people to bankruptcy and made truffles so scarce that armed escorts accompanied them through Paris. I think of those preposterous *pièces montées* of the last century: setpieces of buildings, birds and flowers, made of unlikely combinations of food, costing enormous sums and seldom intended to be eaten. I think of certain dishes definitely meant to be eaten, and here, for a moment, I pause at . . . well, why not at *Côtelettes de Homard Arkangel* in that wide-ranging guide, *Madame Prunier's Fish Cookery Book* (1938):

'Cook a lobster and cut its flesh into dice; mix this with an equal amount of large-grained caviare, and bind with *Mousse de Homard*. When the mixture is set, shape into little cutlets or, simpler still, put the mixture to set in little cutlet-shaped oiled moulds and let it set there. Cover them with *Sauce Chaudfroid* flavoured with a lobster cullis, and then with jelly. Arrange on a dish garnished round the edge with slices of jelly, and hand separately a *Sauce*

Russe.' [This is a mayonnaise to which some of the creamy parts of a lobster and some caviare, both passed through a fine sieve, have been added and which has then been lightly seasoned with French mustard.]

All that remains to be asked is, 'Where are the truffles? Oh, and why wasn't the lobster – as it is in many such recipes – cooked in champagne?'

French cooking can be too elaborate. Nowadays, many of the efforts of the *nouvelle* school seem directed at making it as difficult as possible to achieve a tiny splash of pink, a blob of brown and two watercress leaves in the middle of a plate. But let me, for the moment, return to those lavish years at the end of the last century, and discuss *Sole Otéro*.

SOLE OTÉRO

La Belle Otéro was a courtesan of *la Belle Époque,* the opulent period at the end of the last century and the beginning of this one. She herself was opulent in taste and in figure. Her great rival was another celebrated courtesan, Liane de Pougy, who was very slim. It is related that one evening, at Maxim's, La Belle Otéro, escorted by the obligatory Russian prince, arrived glittering with diamonds from head to foot. Soon after, Liane de Pougy appeared, wearing a plain black dress, and followed by her maid who was covered in as many diamonds as La Belle Otéro.

Soon after hearing this anecdote I came across *Sole Otéro* in Mrs C. F. Leyel's *The Gentle Art of Cookery,* and was moved to study the recipe:

1 small sole
½ pint shrimps, picked
4 large potatoes
butter, pepper, salt

'Choose four large potatoes or as many as are required; they should be chosen to lie well on their sides. Bake them in the oven. When cooked, cut a neat oval in the topmost side of each potato, and scoop out the inside without damaging the skin. Mash up the potato so removed with butter, pepper and salt.

'Cook a small sole. Remove the bones and divide into small pieces. Mix it with half a pint of shrimps and cover the fish with a *Sauce Mornay*. Add the mashed potato and with this mixture refill the cases; replace the end and reheat. Serve them in a silver dish on a napkin.'

I now tracked back to Mrs Leyel's *Sauce Mornay:*

'Prepare a white sauce and, without letting it boil, stir in two tablespoonfuls of grated Parmesan cheese and one ounce of butter added in small pieces. The sauce must be made very hot but must not boil.'

Now I looked up Mrs Leyel's white sauce:

Simple Béchamel Sauce

This sauce is named after the Marquis de Béchamel, who was *maître d'hôtel* to Louis XIV.

'When a sauce is made with flour, it must be allowed to simmer from ten to fifteen minutes after the flour has been added. Otherwise the flour will not be cooked and the sauce will not be at all good.

'To make a *Béchamel Sauce,* melt a piece of butter the size of an egg in a double saucepan, stirring into it, over very gentle heat, two tablespoonfuls of flour. Into this add gradually half a pint of milk, stirring it steadily with a wooden spoon over a slow fire for a quarter of an hour. When it is perfectly smooth and of cream-like consistency, remove from the fire; add salt and pepper, and mix in another smaller piece of butter. This sauce is the basis of all white sauces.'

Considering this dish I found myself confronted by two problems. How on earth was one going to fit all that mashed potato as well as the other ingredients into the cases (even with such a meagre allowance of sole)? And secondly, was this really a dish which would appeal to that diamond-covered lady of *la Belle Époque*? I turned to Madame Prunier:

161

SOLE OTÉRO
(fillets)

'Bake some large waxy potatoes in their jackets, cut a slice off their sides, and remove the pulp. Fill the scooped-out shells three parts full with salpicon of lobster, place in each a folded and poached fillet of sole, cover with Mornay Sauce, and brown quickly in the oven. Put a slice of truffle on each fillet, and serve.'

Yes, that did seem more in La Belle Otéro's style ... much more, and I had to admit that I preferred it myself. Now for Madame Prunier's *Mornay:*

SAUCE MORNAY

'To three-quarters of a pint of *Béchamel Sauce* add, while it is still boiling, a binding of two egg yolks and two ounces of grated Parmesan and Gruyère mixed. Finish with the much reduced cooking liquor of the fish for which the sauce is intended, several spoonfuls of cream and two ounces of butter.' [In my view, the sauce *must* be taken off the boil before the egg yolks are added.]

I was determined to be thorough now that I had become so involved in all this. I took my final step to Madame Prunier's *Béchamel:*

SAUCE BÉCHAMEL

'Mix together four ounces of butter and five of flour and cook this for a few seconds only, just to rid it of the flavour of uncooked flour. Moisten it with three and a half pints of boiled milk, and season it with not quite half an ounce of salt, a pinch of mignonette pepper★ and grated nutmeg, and bring it gently to the boil, stirring all the time. Now add an onion stuck with a clove, a bouquet of parsley, bay leaf and thyme, and let it boil gently for twenty minutes. Then strain it into a bowl, covering the surface with melted butter to prevent a scum from forming.'

I felt quite dazed. What an extraordinary contrast in cooking methods – boiling versus no boiling, the calculation of the time it would take to get rid of the taste of uncooked flour, the addition of egg yolks and cream in the Prunier *Mornay*. But when I thought of eating the finished dish, my preference was absolutely firm. Madame Prunier's won hands down. What Mrs Leyel had made was *Sole Plain Jane*. And this led me to rethink some of my strictures on French elaboration. Very often it is well worth while, though all that cholesterol is so much against today's rules.

Note: When Maxim's, which opened in 1893, celebrated their fiftieth anniversary in 1949 (they did not count the war years), both Otéro and de Pougy were present. History, alas, does not relate what they wore. But it does relate that de Pougy married a Rumanian prince, and was very rich to the end of her life when, widowed, she entered a convent and became a nun. Otéro, on the other hand, died in classic, *La Bohème* poverty, with a few sticks of furniture in a genuine garret. I don't know quite what the moral of this story is.

★Mignonette pepper is ordinary white pepper.

Despite my yielding to the blandishments of classic rich French cooking in the previous recipe, to me, of all the scents and savours which arise in a kitchen where French cuisine is in practice, the most stimulating and alluring is that of the humble mussel which – thank heaven – still remains a comparatively cheap luxury. The old quart measurement of around twenty mussels – approximately 550g (1¼lb) – is, for me, a minimum ration per head when I am contemplating a dish of *Moules Marinière,* one of the very simplest and most satisfying of dishes. Although I have given recipes for this elsewhere, I could not contemplate writing any book about food which did not include it.

MOULES MARINIÈRE
Mussels Marinière

Serves 3

1.5kg (3¾lb) mussels, rigorously checked and cleaned, the outer part of the byssus, or beard, removed in each case

150ml (¼ pint) white wine

600ml (1 pint) water

1 dessertspoon chopped chives *or* 1 small onion, finely chopped

2 sprigs fennel (fresh or dried)

1 small bay leaf

1 dessertspoon fresh thyme *or* 1 teaspoon dried

2 pinches salt

2 pinches ground black pepper

1 tablespoon chopped parsley

Into a large, deep, lidded cooking pot, put the wine and water, and all the ingredients except the mussels. Now slip the mussels in carefully so as not to break any shells. Shake them down comfortably. On a brisk fire, bring to the boil, and let the mussels cook for 1 minute in the steam generated. Shake the pan and boil for another minute. Remove the pan from the heat and give it one good final shake: the mussels should now all be open and disgorging their delicious juices into the savoury *bouillon*. Cover them and let them stand for a minute longer, while this process goes on. Lift the mussels out and distribute them in deep, hot soup-plates. Ladle the *bouillon* over the mussels, scatter parsley on top, and serve with crusty French bread.

Note: Variations on the generally accepted version of this dish are many, but I would say that any version which tends to thicken the liquid – with *Béchamel*, eggs or cream – turns the resultant dish into something other than what a true *Marinière* is meant to be: that is, a simple distillation of the exquisite juices of the mussel, enhanced by the herbs and seasonings in the wine-and-water *bouillon*. I have chosen this recipe to represent what is simplest and best in French cooking – and exactly to my own personal taste.

The *à la meunière* method of shallow-frying – or, rather, sauté-ing – is another example of the pre-excellence of simple French cooking. The method, when applied to scallops, brings out the flavour of that delicious bivalve as does no other.

COQUILLES SAINT-JACQUES À LA MEUNIÈRE
Scallops Meunière

For a main dish you will probably need three scallops per person.

scallops
a small saucer of milk
flour, seasoned with salt and black pepper
clarified butter (see below), about 75g (3oz) for 3 scallops
1 tablespoon fine breadcrumbs (for 3 scallops)
for garnish
1 dessertspoon parsley, finely chopped

Your scallops will have been opened by the fishmonger. Remove and discard the 'skirts'. Now cut the white body of the scallop horizontally into 3 pieces and brush these with milk. Repeat this process with the orange coral 'cocks'-combs'. Roll all pieces over a board sprinkled with seasoned flour.

Melt 50g (2oz) of clarified butter in a frying pan. Put the scallop pieces in this, to cook gently for 4–5 minutes on each side, until they begin to take colour. Remove them to a warm dish. Add the remaining butter to the pan and scatter the breadcrumbs in it. Stir them round and let them cook for a minute. When the butter just begins to brown, pour the contents of the pan over the pieces of scallop in the dish. Sprinkle with the parsley and serve.

Clarified butter

For a long time I believed, like many other people (including such an authority as Constance Spry), that clarifying butter merely meant removing the salt. I was wrong and, in fact, when clarifying butter nowadays, I use unsalted butter, about 450g (1lb) each time. Clarifying butter gets rid of water, buttermilk and any other 'foreign matter' which, when you are frying, makes the butter blacken and burn. It also causes the butter to solidify as it cools, making it an excellent agent for 'sealing'. In India (where it is known as *ghee*) and in the Middle East, butter is almost invariably clarified for cooking (unless modern methods of refrigeration are available). The reason for this is because clarifying prevents butter from becoming rancid.

Method: Put the butter in a large frying pan. Let it melt over a very low heat (it should *not* brown) until it bubbles. Remove it from the heat and leave it for a minute or two. While it is still warm, pour it through a piece of butter-muslin or cheesecloth, wrung out in warm water and lining a sieve placed over your storage jar. Keep the clarified butter in a jar in the refrigerator.

Still in search of simplicity and perfection, to represent French cooking at its best, from my personal point of view, my mind turns inevitably to that most French and peasantly of southern *ragoûts* or vegetable stews: the *ratatouille*. This, though patently not a fish dish itself, I would choose and cherish as an accompaniment to any non-oily fish, poached or grilled and eaten either hot or cold.

167

RATATOUILLE
Aromatic Vegetable Stew

Serves 4 or 5

2 medium-sized aubergines

salt

3 medium-sized onions, finely chopped

4 tablespoons virgin olive oil

3 red and 3 green sweet peppers, seeded,
de-pithed and sliced into rings

4 large tomatoes, peeled and quartered

2 cloves garlic, crushed

1 teaspoon freshly ground black pepper

First cut the unskinned aubergines into sizeable chunks. Put them into a colander and sprinkle them liberally with salt. Allow them to drain for an hour; this will remove the first bitter exudations of the vegetable. Wash them well to remove the salt. Now put the onions into the heated oil in a saucepan, to stew slowly until soft but not brown. Add the aubergines and the peppers, and let them cook for about 10 minutes. Add the tomatoes, the crushed garlic and the black pepper. Cover the pan, and let all gently stew together for at least another 25 minutes. Serve hot or cold.

Note: This is a basic *ratatouille*. Some people include other ingredients, such as artichoke hearts and courgettes. There is also an élitist school of thought which prescribes that each of the ingredients should be cooked separately and only amalgamated at the end. Provided the vegetables are added to allow different cooking times and not all put into the oil together at the beginning, I see no justification for this refinement.

Now memory takes over again as I recall my convalescence in Menton after that gruesome tonsillectomy in Nice which I have already described. The hotel I was staying at was insecure: in the sense that every high tide brought a foot of seawater flooding into the dining-room. (Those who believe that the Mediterranean is a tideless sea should think again.)

One evening it was low tide, and we were able to go down to dinner. 'Tonight,' said the *maître d'hôtel,* with considerable unction, 'we have *Saint-Pierre.*' 'Good,' we replied, wondering whether the Pope had arrived, and sat down.

After we had enjoyed four or five tiny sepia fish, egged, breadcrumbed and fried, the *Saint-Pierre* was served: two beautiful fillets apiece, vaguely quadrilateral in shape and exquisitely rounded at the edges. They were of a brilliant whiteness, such as is only to be found in the glazes used by Della Robbia in his Florentine terracottas. This *Saint-Pierre,* we call John Dory. In Cyprus it is known as *Christopsaro* (Christ's fish) and in Greece as *Aghios Petros* (St Peter, again). It has become a favourite of mine not only because it is fairly regularly available but because of its most exceptional and individual flavour, which excels that of sole.

It was years after I had eaten *Saint-Pierre* at Menton that I saw one of these most exciting of fish, whole and in the flesh, and immediately recognised the strong relationship it has with Picasso's cubist portraits of women. Sadness and disillusionment are common to both, but there was nothing *triste* to be found in the dish of fillets I ate so long ago in Menton. Dressed, as they were, with true Gallic discretion, they boasted no complicated sauce: just a simple blending of the *jus de cuisson* of the poached fillets themselves with the *coulis* from large mussels (opened just seconds before the dish was served, and so still discharging their goodness), supported only by small, melting pats of Chive Butter.

SAINT-PIERRE AUX MOULES
John Dory with Mussels

the 4 fillets from a John Dory,
weighing about 1kg (2¼lb)

600ml (1 pint) *court-bouillon* (double the
quantities of the one given on page 45)

1 glass white wine,
if additional liquid required

12 mussels

Chive Butter (made by kneading 50g
(2oz) butter with 1 tablespoon of finely
chopped chives, and seasoned with a few
drops of lemon juice and a sprinkling of
freshly ground black pepper; add a pinch
of salt if you are using unsalted butter)

In the smallest flat pan that will hold your fillets, fitted cosily together, put your *court-bouillon,* and bring it to simmering point. Slide the fillets in. (If the *bouillon* does not quite cover them, add a glass of white wine.) Cook for 12 minutes. As the fillets poach, spoon the bubbling liquid over them. Put the cooked fillets on a heated serving dish.

Now put the mussels in a heavy pan with not more than a ladleful of the *court-bouillon.* Cook briskly until all the mussels are open (this should not take more than 1½ minutes). As soon as they are open, lift them out and place them around the fish fillets, on each of which you should put a 12g (½oz) pat of the Chive Butter. Spoon over the dish 2 tablespoons of the liquid from the pan in which the mussels were opened. Serve at once.

The rise in price and prestige of the *lotte de mer,* or monkfish, is of great personal interest to me, as I have long been one of its greatest admirers. Fifteen years ago, in the course of a panegyric upon it, I rejoiced that it was at 'the lower end of the price-range' and added that my only dread was that the discovery of its qualities might make it fashionable for restaurant dishes. My dread has been fully justified by subsequent events, and the monkfish is now priced among the aristocracy of fish, despite its hideous appearance (though fishmongers almost invariably remove the head before displaying it). This hideous appearance, however, provides the foundation for a delightful historico-theatrical anecdote.

In 1905, 'the divine' Sarah Bernhardt and Stella (Mrs Patrick) Campbell appeared together in Sarah's production of Maeterlinck's play, *Pelléas et Mélisande.* Stella complained bitterly that a fountain into which she was meant to gaze in the second act was nothing but a 'silly fishpond'. One evening, Sarah sent a messenger to acquire the most hideous fish she could find and install it in the 'fountain'. When Stella gazed dreamily down into the stone basin, she saw . . . a monkfish. She began to shake with laughter; it was several seconds before she could manage to speak her first line, which was, *'Je voudrais toucher l'eau'* ('I would like to touch the water'). Sarah had had her revenge for the remark about the 'silly fishpond'.

Here is a simple recipe which returns us to the innocent days of the *Béchamel,* and does not disguise the unique flavour of this noble fish.

LOTTE AU FOUR
Monkfish, Cooked in the Oven

Serves 4–6

3 medium-sized onions, finely chopped

225g (8oz) mushrooms

2 small carrots, grated

1 dessertspoon celery, finely chopped

100g (4oz) butter
1 whole monkfish tail, skinned and weighing about 1kg (2¼lb)
300ml (½ pint) *Béchamel,* made according to the recipe on page 96
2 tablespoons dry white wine
1 teaspoon freshly ground black pepper
2 good pinches salt
2 tablespoons fine breadcrumbs
25g (1oz) melted butter
1 dessertspoon parsley, finely chopped

In a pan, cook the onions, half the mushrooms, the grated carrots and the celery in 50g (2oz) of the butter. Pound them, as they cook, with a wooden spoon, until they almost meld together. Now, with a sharp knife, cut down the spine of the monkfish tail. Let the knife reach the bone, so that a small separation occurs between it and the flesh on either side. Now lay the cooked vegetables in the bottom of a large baking dish. Put the fish on top of them. Cover the dish with foil, and put it in a preheated moderate oven (Gas 4/180°C/350°F) for 25 minutes.

At this juncture, take the dish out of the oven. It will be seen that the gap on either side of the main bone will have widened and that the flesh is now on the point of springing away from it. Encourage this with your knife, and remove the main bone.

Enrich your *Béchamel* by folding in the remaining 2oz (50g) of butter, the remaining mushrooms, puréed raw, and the white wine. Season the sauce and pour over the fish, making sure that it fills the gap in the centre. Cover with the breadcrumbs and then sprinkle with the melted butter, followed by the chopped parsley.

Raise the oven temperature to Gas 6/200°C/400°F. Replace the baking dish in the oven (without the foil this time) and cook until nicely brown. Serve from the baking dish.

By the way, the running battle of onstage fish jokes between Sarah Bernhardt and Stella Campbell continued when they took *Pelléas et Mélisande* on tour. Its climax came during one performance when Sarah had to reach up to caress Stella's hair. Under the cover of her long tresses, Stella slipped a live goldfish into Sarah's hand. (Completely calm, Sarah kept the goldfish in her fist for the rest of the scene.)

Goldfish is one fish I am definitely not prepared to cook. There is another.

MORUE
Dried Salt Cod

I have always been baffled by the chic charm this survival food seems to hold for many excellent cookery writers. (I was recently delighted, reading Claudia Roden's splendid *Mediterranean Cookery,* to find that she shares my opinion, graphically describing the smelly tedium of its preparation.)

Salt cod is a relic of a period when fish supplies were strictly seasonal, and refrigeration and transport of fresh fish impossible. It was – in my view most appropriately – an integral part of penitential *maigre* fare in Lent. I have here decided, as a form of protest, to provide no recipes for it, and instead to quote some verses by my wife's late mother, Milla Cavendish, which I found in the back of one of her books, attached to a column from *The Times* of 28 April 1939, headed 'Recipes for Small Households' and giving instructions for Salt Cod with Eggs, Salt Cod with Black Butter, Salt Cod *à la Cardinal,* Salt Cod Fish Balls, Salt Cod *à la Lyonnaise* and Salt Cod *à la Creole.*

O Father *Times,* please think again,
Before you give your readers pain.

If Household's small and means are mod,
Why add a burden of 'SALT COD'?

To see SALT COD upon your page
'Puts all Heaven in a rage'.

Heaven avert 'SALT COD Fish Balls'
In April when the cuckoo calls.

'SALT COD *à la Lyonnaise'*
Afflicts the heart with its malaise.

Why should I need to live at all
To eat 'SALT COD *à la Cardinal'*?

I'd sooner drink a can of Vitriol
Than eat 'SALT COD *à la Creole'.*

I'll sink beneath the ready sod
Before I touch or eat 'SALT COD'.

Cyprus

Limassol has now been my happy home for more than ten years and, though its supplies and varieties of fish are limited (and, in comparison to other foods, expensive), and I cannot help brooding on the fish – such as oysters, mussels and the crab – I left behind me, I have succeeded in coming to terms with the fish situation in a variety of ways.

At one time I thought that the British – with the exception of their introduction of the ubiquitous chips – had little influence on Cypriot cooking. I am not altogether sure, on mature reflection, that this is true. The vegetables accompanying steak, chops or weighty (pork) 'schnitzels' will invariably consist of a mixture of tinned peas and tinned carrots (this in an island which is a vegetable paradise!), and I have never been offered potatoes in any form except chips (with the one exception of the 'roast' potatoes, cooked till soft in a mixture of oil and water, which accompany the Sunday joint). Soups, too, invariably turn out to be tinned, apart from *avgolemono* (of which more later) and – but you will only find this in private houses – *trahana,* made from dried slices of wheat and sour milk (it sounds alarming, but it is actually interesting and delicious) and *patsha,* the sheep's head soup served late at night in various dives in the 'cabaret' district . . .

Perhaps the real British influence is to be found in a nervousness of rich, strongly seasoned dishes. (Paradoxically it seems that, apart from a shrinking band of peasants, the English are now the only people in Cyprus who eat garlic, which is considered unrefined by the burgeoning middle-class.) Hotel and 'smart' restaurant dishes tend to be insipid, though of course this is the case all over the world where tourists are catered for with so-called 'international' food.

However, there is a peasant tradition of good slow cooking of meat and vegetables, with oil, and there are also some interesting smoked meats, and sausages such as the well-known *sheftalia,* grilled for kebabs. Unfortunately, from my point of view, all these dishes have one disadvantage. None of them involves fish . . .

On the whole, Cyprus fish cookery is exceedingly plain. Fish is either fried (usually, I am glad to say, in a very thin batter, as opposed to the dreadful blanket of most English fish-and-chip shops) or grilled. (If you are eating a fish meal in a restaurant, you can specify that it should be grilled.) The fish is always accompanied by wedges of lemon, and bottles of olive oil and lemon juice are on the table. What could be healthier, or more delicious, than fresh fish served in this way? How noble is the climax of a 'Full Fish *mezé*', when, after various dishes of small fish, the Big Fish is served forth on its platter. It has been scaled, and then grilled on both sides. Then it has been split open down the back, and its flesh anointed with a mixture of oil and lemon juice, after which it has been covered with a layer of coarsely chopped Mediterranean parsley. And yet . . . sometimes I yearn – perhaps you will say corruptly? – for variation and elaboration.

No sauces are ever produced. (*Tahina* and *taramasalata* which, at a – rather sharp – pinch, could be classified as sauces are served, with bread and salad, as a first course, not with the fish.)

Only in the case of the cephalopods – octopus, squid, cuttlefish – is the treatment sometimes more adventurous. In a *mezé*, pickled octopus or squid is often included. And though the most usual way of serving squid is battered and fried (the tiny *kalamarakia* can be delicious, but I am afraid I always rudely refer to the large, tough and rather tasteless rings of *kalamaria* as 'bicycle tyres'), they are also made into stews, with wine.

There are no 'fishermen's soups' in Cyprus (I think it must be the only Mediterranean country where this is the case). However there is one fish soup, a variant of the *avgolemono,* where fish stock replaces the chicken stock of the usual version. I have not often come across this soup and have not been able to find a satisfactory local recipe for it, so I have produced my own version, following the *avgolemono* method, but using fish commonly available in England.

AVGOLEMONO PSARASOUPA
Fish, Egg and Lemon Soup

Serves 6–7

450g (1lb) fillets whiting, cod, hake, haddock or coley

2 litres (3½ pints) rich fish stock (see page 113)

6 tablespoons long-grain rice

2 eggs

1 tablespoon medium-dry white wine

juice of 2 lemons
salt and pepper to taste
for garnish
2 tablespoons parsley, finely chopped

Poach the fish fillets in the strained stock for 6 or 7 minutes. Remove it from the stock to a dish, and cut into small – 15g (½oz) – pieces. Set aside to cool. Now put the rice into the stock and cook quickly until tender. Remove from the heat to cool down. Meanwhile beat the eggs, wine and lemon juice together. Add to this a ladleful of the stock and beat well. Incorporate this mixture into the body of the stock. Add the pieces of fish and season with pepper and salt. Replace the soup on the fire and make piping hot, but *do not allow it to boil*. At the last minute, just before serving, shower in the parsley. Ladle into heated soup bowls and serve at once.

BARBOUNIA KRASATA
Red Mullet in Wine

Serves 4–6

Plaintive as I am about the absence of sauces in Cypriot fish cookery, I was most interested to discover the following Cyprus recipe in Arto der Haroutunian's highly informative *Middle Eastern Cookery*. He describes it as 'particularly good' - and he's right!

900g (2lb) red mullet, entrails removed
olive oil

Wine Sauce

300ml (½ pint) dry white wine
3 cloves garlic, crushed
1 tablespoon tomato purée
2 tablespoons parsley, finely chopped
1 teaspoon dried tarragon
25g (1oz) dry breadcrumbs
1 teaspoon salt
½ teaspoon black pepper
½ teaspoon fennel

'Cut the fins off the fish. Wash thoroughly inside and out.

'Line a large baking dish with silver foil, leaving enough to fold over and cover the fish. Brush the foil with olive oil and place the fish in the dish.

'In a bowl mix together the wine, garlic and tomato purée and then add the parsley, tarragon and breadcrumbs. Sprinkle the fish with the salt, pepper and fennel and then pour in the wine sauce. Fold the foil over to seal in the fish. Bake in an oven preheated to Gas 5/190°C/375°F, for 25–30 minutes or until the fish is tender and flakes easily. Remove the dish from the oven and carefully lift the fish on to a serving dish. Pour the sauce over the top and garnish with a little parsley.'

In the two recipes that follow I have adapted two Cyprus dishes, which are normally made with minced meat, for use with fish. To my mind, this is an improvement: in any case, I think you will find them worth eating.

SEPIA SHEFTALIA LASSALLE
Cuttlefish Sausages Lassalle

These can also be described as cuttlefish *andouillettes* or sausages.

Novelties in Cyprus cookery are not to be expected and one *Yiayia's* (Granny's) octopus stew is much like another, give or take a blade of mace or a sprig of thyme. So I have been moved, with the cooperation of a friend of ours, Mrs Androula Costi, to attempt a small adventure – no less an adventure than the invention of a fish sausage!

The normal *sheftalia* is a small sausage-shaped parcel of minced lamb, well seasoned, spiced and herbed, and wrapped in the finest 'frilly' (the term is Jane Grigson's) mesentery of the sheep or pig. (Bought cleaned, these are in no way distasteful, resembling sheets of transparent paper.) The *sheftalia* are then slid, 3 or 4 at a time, on to a spit, and grilled until very and beautifully brown. Folded into heated pitta or Arab bread, this is one of the really good 'takeaways' Cyprus provides.

The following recipe for cuttlefish *andouillettes,* or *sepia* sausage, should be of interest to far-sighted Cypriot and Greek restaurateurs in England, as well as to the home cook. Those who have tasted them here – and I include Cypriot families with children – have pronounced them delicious.

This quantity makes 16–18 *andouillettes* and will serve six to eight people as a first course, or as a main course accompanied by salad and pitta bread.

2kg (4½lb) *sepia* (cuttlefish)
the crumbs of 4 thick slices fresh white bread
1 full teaspoon salt
2 teaspoons freshly ground black pepper
3 medium-sized onions, chopped
4 cloves, ground
2 sticks cinnamon
1 blade mace
2 small leaves sage
2 good sprigs parsley
1 sprig thyme
1½ dessertspoons virgin olive oil
1 large whole fresh egg
length of fine 'frilly' mesentery (called *panna* in Cyprus)
olive oil, lemon juice and seasoning, for basting

Remove the cuttle shell, tentacles and ink-sacs, and discard. Chop the cuttlefish coarsely. With your hands break up the crumb of the slices of bread. Now put all the ingredients into a food processor and blend together. Transfer the mixture to a large bowl and, with the hands, knead it well together. It should not be too sticky or loose to form into one large ball.

Now put the bowl on the upper shelf of your refrigerator for half an hour. This will help to make the texture sufficiently stiff. If the mixture shows signs of crumbling, add *just 3 drops* of olive oil. Knead again, then replace in the refrigerator for another hour.

Now, with the hands, form the mixture into portions (7cm/3in × 5cm/2in) shaped like small fat torpedos.

Lay a length of the fine 'frilly' mesentery (15cm/6in wide) on a clean flat surface. Place your torpedo-shaped filling in the middle and roll it a half-turn, bringing the edge of the mesentery up with it to half-cover the dough. Fold up the mesentery on each side of the 'parcel'. Roll the 'parcel' forward again a half-turn, and with a sharp knife cut off the fine clinging material to produce a neat plump *andouillette*.

The fine mesentery casing is strong, and the *andouillettes* should be spitted and grilled (far preferably over charcoal) until they are a deep and glistening 'burnt umber' all over, when the filling should be thoroughly cooked all through. As they cook, they can be basted with a brush dipped in a saucer of olive oil and lemon juice, pepper and salt, beaten together.

SIPIOPSOMO LASSALLE
Cuttlefish Loaf Lassalle

This makes a marvellous dish for roasting in the oven, to be served in slices for Sunday lunch. It can also be served cold. In addition, if you find mesentery difficult to obtain, or simply do not want to be bothered with it, you can bake the mixture in an oiled loaf tin, brushing the top of the fish loaf with olive oil, lemon juice, salt and pepper. However, if enclosed in a sheet of mesentery, the mixture will be easier to slice and the whole of its exterior will be browned.

To make this splendid loaf, use the same ingredients as for the previous recipe, simply doubling the quantities of all of them, including the fish. Form into one large cylindrical roll and wrap in a sheet of mesentery. The roll should be put in a baking tin in the oven (preheated to Gas 6/200°C/400°F) and baked for 1 hour. Basting from time to time with the oil and lemon mixture already described is recommended.

If you are not using the mesentery, the mixture will of course be shaped to the loaf tin, as when making a meat loaf.

MUSSELS IRENE STREET
(faute de mieux)

The two recipes that follow are certainly not Cypriot. However, they are part of our life in Cyprus and have evolved from Cyprus conditions, so that I feel they belong in this section. Both taste very good, and I think could certainly be found useful in Britain at that time of the year when – though there is no scientific justification for this – fresh mussels are definitely not obtainable.

My wife shares my love for the divine bivalve which I describe as 'the truffle of the sea', and to raise an echo of it ('mixing memory and desire'), she has invented these two dishes, using tinned Danish mussels. (NB Mussels *au naturel* – tinned in brine – MUST be used: NOT those tinned in vinegar.)

COLD MUSSEL SOUP

Serves 6

This is about as 'instant' as a soup can be. Like the succeeding recipe, it involves a food processor. The cream is tinned because fresh cream in Limassol must be ordered in advance, unless a pilgrimage is made to a distant grocer in the tourist area, and tends anyway to be very thin, even when called 'double'. In Britain, cream is not always present in the refrigerator of every home, and if a 'sudden soup' is wanted, UHT or Long Life cream (which keeps for up to a month) can be useful to have at hand. In this dish, the strong flavour of the mussels overcomes any shortcomings in that of the cream.

the leaves of a small bunch of parsley
2 × 250g (8.8oz) tins Danish mussels in brine
2 shallots *or* 1 small onion
1 × 170g (5½oz) tin cream, which has been kept in the refrigerator *or* 200ml (7fl. oz) UHT or Long Life cream
up to 300ml (½ pint) milk

Put the parsley in to the food processor, and using the metal blade, grind fine. Remove one dessertspoonful to use as a garnish. Now add the mussels, with the liquid they are canned in, the shallots or onion and the cream. Process to a thick purée. Dilute the soup with milk to a creamy consistency. Chill. Serve garnished with a little parsley.

MUSSEL AND SPINACH PANCAKES WITH TWO SAUCES

Serves 4–6

This is a much more elaborate recipe, but again, its making is eased by the food processor. (In Cyprus, in the summer months, a disinclination to spend many hours cooking cannot be dismissed as 'laziness'.)

for the pancakes

300ml (½ pint) milk

1 egg

½ teaspoon salt

100g (4oz) plain flour

25–50g (1–2oz) butter

for the filling

3 good bunches spinach

1 small onion, blanched

1–2 tins Danish mussels in brine, 250g (8.8oz), drained weight 150g (6oz)

½ teaspoon freshly ground black pepper

Tomato Sauce

500g (1lb) fresh tomatoes

1 seeded green pepper, blanched

a good pinch of salt

450ml (¾ pint) Mornay Sauce
(see pages 162–3)

for topping

25g (1oz) Parmesan cheese, finely grated

25g (1oz) Gruyère cheese, finely grated

Process all the pancake ingredients, except the butter. Leave the batter to stand for half an hour.

Cook the spinach in 2.5cm (1in) boiling salted water for 3–4 minutes. Drain. (I usually do this by putting the spinach in a colander and pressing it with a large stone – from the birthplace of the goddess Aphrodite, near Paphos. I then squeeze it in my hands.) Blanch the onion. Drain the mussels. Process all these ingredients together, with the pepper.

Cook the pancakes (the quantities given should make 8–10). For the best results – to obtain thin, light, lacy pancakes – use as little butter as possible – just enough to grease the pan.

Fill the pancakes with the mussel and spinach mixture, rolling them neatly and arranging them in a *very* lightly buttered ovenproof dish.

Process the tomatoes, peeled and seeded, with the blanched green pepper, and the salt. Pour this over and around the pancakes. (If you must, use canned peeled tomatoes, but the flavour, to me, is inferior.)

Now make the Mornay Sauce. Pour over the whole surface of the dish. Sprinkle with the cheeses, and put in the oven until thoroughly heated and golden brown on top.

Note: If covered with foil, and with the topping of grated cheese omitted, this dish can be kept in the refrigerator overnight. Next day, when required, sprinkle with the cheese and heat as before.

I feel that it would be appropriate to leave the subject of cooking in Cyprus with a final tribute – in local-recipe form – to the splendid cephalopod. Once he has you in his clutches – perhaps this metaphor is unfortunate – you will never be able to escape. It is his unfamiliarity that alarms you, but once you get over your initial shyness, you will find him a staunch culinary ally – even a kitchen pet. To me, the octopus, the squid and – especially – the cuttlefish are essential elements of the Mediterranean experience which has always played such a large rôle in my cookery and my life. They are natural partners of those other Mediterranean staples: garlic, olive oil, red wine. And the kitchen from which these are absent seems to me a pallid, bloodless place, rather resembling Homer's description of the Halls of Hades where 'mere shadows flit to and fro'.

OKTOPODI YAHNI
Octopus Stew

Serves 6–8

1kg (2 ½lb) octopus, with its beak, eyes and ink-sac removed (your fishmonger will do this for you)

3 large Spanish onions, chopped small

½ tumbler strong red wine

½ tumbler dry white wine

3 bay leaves

3 cinnamon sticks

4 cloves

5 black peppercorns, crushed	
1 large clove garlic, crushed	
1 tablespoon tomato purée	
3 tablespoons virgin olive oil	
salt to taste	

Put the octopus in the stewing pan. Cover with water and bring briskly to the boil and simmer for 20 minutes. Drain and wash thoroughly in cold water. Cut up into small pieces and put back in a clean stewpot. Cover with water and add all the other ingredients except the olive oil and the salt. Allow to boil briskly for 15 minutes. Now reduce heat until the liquid is down to simmering point. Add the olive oil. Let all simmer as slowly as possible until most of the liquid has gone. (Cooking octopus is a long job and 4–5 hours should be allowed.) Now season with salt to taste, and serve with thick chunks of village bread. (The round crusty Cyprus loaf is now available in most English cities.)

KALAMARAKIA YAHNI
Squid Stew

Follow the above recipe, substituting squid for octopus. The first boiling and subsequent draining and washing are unnecessary, there being no dubious initial exudations from the skin of squid. As with the octopus, very slow cooking is important, but the squid will usually be found to be tender after only 1 hour's very slow simmering.

SOUPIES YAHNI
Cuttlefish Stew

In the last few years I have come to regard the *sepia,* or cuttlefish, as the best-flavoured fish in the cephalopod group. It has indeed an exquisite flavour and makes tender eating without necessarily – unless it is very large – having to be cooked for hours and hours, like the octopus. I have heard that, in England, cuttlefish is the hardest to obtain of the cephalopods. But persevere – it is worth the effort.

The ingredients for this stew are the same as those used in the two recipes above, except that (though you should discard the head of the cuttlefish) you should preserve two ink-sacs.

As with squid, the initial boiling, draining and washing are not necessary.

The cooking method is the same as in the previous recipes except that, when the liquid has been reduced, through simmering, by one-third, you should put in the broken ink-sacs. Allow to cook slowly until the liquid – by now a most intriguing Goya-esque colour – is three-quarters gone.

6
A LAST WORD ON THE FIRST COURSE

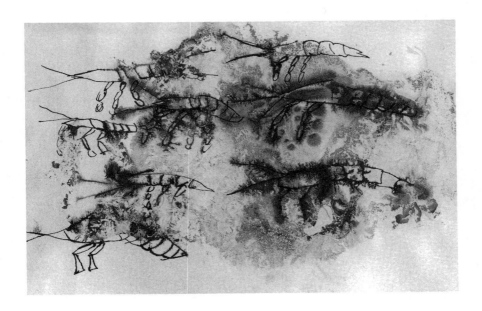

The first shall be last . . . This seems to me perfectly natural, since I am a life-long practitioner of inverse, as opposed to lateral, thinking.

Excluding, of course, soup, the first course – hot or cold – was always referred to as the *'hors-d'oeuvre'* until some time in the 1960s when it became known as the 'starter'. The change from a complex foreign term to a simple English one is obviously sensible. I approve, and yet, for me, the word still has frightening associations with unsatisfactory restaurants bearing names such as Chompers, Champers, Munchers and Noshers. Hence my title-reference to the First Course.

It was Lord Curzon, Viceroy of India and later Foreign Secretary (immortalised in the lines, 'My name is George Nathaniel Curzon. I am a most superior person'), who made the pronouncement that 'a gentleman never has soup at luncheon', and even after the Second World War, *hors-d'oeuvre* – in circles in which I did not move – were not (with the sole exception of oysters or caviare) served at dinner. How pleasant it is that now even the most exalted can enjoy a fish soup at either noon or night, and also that, when the mood takes them, and particularly before a well-sauced main dish, they can replace it, at dinner, with a more piquantly contrasting first course.

You will perhaps have noticed, in the preceding pages, a trend towards simplicity: a rejection, in most cases, of excessive elaboration in cookery. My thinking about the first course is along the same lines. I do not want to engage in proceedings such as those involved in the creation of *Côtelettes de Homard Arkangel* (see page 159). At the same time, I rebel against a new tyranny: I refuse to create edible Japanese paintings on plates; an activity often quite as time-consuming as the routines of the old *haute cuisine*. I am always keen for food to look nice, but if you want instructions for making roses out of smoked salmon, or 'poached eggs' from small circles of turbot, each with a quail's egg at its centre, or tiny *millefeuilles* containing intricate mousses and bordered with three differently coloured sauces, or vegetable garnishes sculpted into the shapes of a variety of fish (I could extend this list almost indefinitely): I am not your man. You must seek out those artist-decorators of – literally – our interiors: the new Great Chefs.

I hope that my inclination towards simplicity will not be taken as evidence of puritanism. Listing my favourite simple first courses, I come up with the following:

1 75–100g (3–4oz) Beluga (or Sevruga will do) caviare, with lemon juice and thin brown bread and butter.

2 A dozen Whitstable Natives (or large Colchesters), with the same accompaniments as the caviare.

3 100g (4oz) of the best Scotch smoked salmon, sliced wafer-thin. The same accompaniments as above, except that I would add a drop or two of Tabasco sauce, which I would 'spread' over the salmon with the aid of the lemon juice.

4 75g (3oz) *avgotarakho* (see page 131), again sliced wafer-thin, with brown bread and butter but, in this case, no lemon.

5 *Moules Marinière* (see page 164) with good crusty French bread.

Note: Nowadays I shudder at the thought of plovers' or quails' eggs, but I am less sure about my attitude to gulls' eggs (which taste so deliciously fishy that they almost count as fish). Surely these strident scavengers are not an endangered species? Should an opportunity of enjoying this delicacy ever again present itself (which I doubt) I shall consult an ecologist. It used to be 'the thing' to serve the blue eggs (bought ready-boiled from the fishmonger) in a nest of moss, accompanied by powdered rock-salt mixed with paprika and – inevitably – thin slices of brown bread and butter.

Returning from what is – for me – largely a trip down nostalgia alley, let us examine the many attractive alternatives to the luxuries I have listed above (though, of course, one of them, *Moules Marinière* is still not a luxury as far as cost is concerned).

Cold First Courses

I live in a Mediterranean climate and, considering cold first courses, I was suddenly 'troubled by doubts' about British cooks' (and eaters') equal enthusiasm for them. On reflection, I think these doubts are quite unjustified. First of all – one real sign of 'progress' – British houses are now kept at a comfortable temperature (no need to jostle for position round the fire). Indeed, my wife, who hates the cold, has decided that, climatically, the ideal time to visit England is in the winter when most interiors are 'lovely and warm'. It is in May and June, when the central heating has been turned off by the hardy natives, that Mediterranean visitors tend to shiver. (Nonetheless I think cold *soup* can seem rather an unfriendly beginning to a February meal, and I do believe that, in general, during winter, the main course should be hot.)

The advantages to the cook, preparing a three-course meal, of a cold first – and third – course are obvious. She/he may well be out at work all day, and cold courses and their constituents are usually more easily readied in advance (ie, the night before). In most cases, nowadays, cooking and serving the meal must be a solo performance. Even when a steel-true partner is keen to help, someone must talk to guests and perform the vital task of refilling their glasses. When the flanking courses are cold, the cook-hostess, or -host, need not be hot or harassed, and the social *Swan Lake* can be danced with far more aplomb.

Turning the pages the other day of that renowned (and, in my view, often extremely unreliable) encyclopaedia, the *Larousse Gastronomique*, I was interested to find some hints on the presentation of cold *hors-d'oeuvre*.

(1) *The dishes.* Apart from special *hors-d'oeuvre* sets, china or glass plates and dishes or antique gold or silver plate may be used.

Old rustic-style plates, pottery or silver porringers, crystal bowls, etc, can be used very effectively.

(2) *The garnishes.* Garnishes, though purely decorative, *must all be edible*.

So, by all means, bring out the family gold plate. I am afraid that rustic-style plates and pottery porringers are more in my line. And I am in absolute agreement that you should not decorate your food with shells, sequins, oleander leaves or the pretty purple flowers of belladonna.

Smoked fish

Apart from salmon, there are, of course, various other fish which are delicious smoked, and ideal for first courses: eel, mackerel and trout particularly. At one time, I was constantly mashing up these delicacies with butter or cream cheese, anchovy fillets, lemon juice and a variety of seasonings to make pâtés or, as I know I should call them, 'pastes'. (It is no use. When I try to use that word a phantom phalanx of little glass jars bearing romantic legends such as 'Sardine and Tomato' forms before my eyes, and I begin to stammer.)

Nowadays I prefer to eat smoked fish plainly filleted with – you have guessed rightly – lemon juice and brown bread and butter. Sometimes I add a little red or freshly ground black pepper. In the case of smoked trout and smoked mackerel, a touch of creamed horseradish can make a piquant change.

I am always pleased when visitors from England bring me *Patum Peperium*, the Gentleman's Relish, whether in a china or a plastic container.

The only 'spread' I make, using what I would call 'first-class' fish, is the cod's-roe version of *Tarama* given on page 131. Otherwise, I sometimes put together what I find to be agreeable mixtures based on bottled or tinned ingredients.

Lumpfish roe

Very early in the 1970s, dining at the house of a (superb) cook, I was confronted by a startling new first course: a refrigerated sherry glass of jellied (Crosse & Blackwell's) consommé, topped with a dollop of whipped cream, lavishly sprinkled with black lumpfish 'caviare'. I enjoyed it. On several occasions, when time was scarce, I served it under my own roof. I would be too cowardly to do so today, for this recipe has become the butt of comic novelists and newspaper columnists. I wonder why. Perhaps because it is so easy.

I have, however, found another purpose for lumpfish roe. (You can use either the red or the black, but the red definitely looks prettier.)

1 × 50g (2oz) jar lumpfish roe
1 × 200g (4oz) Philadelphia (or similar) cream cheese
2 shallots, finely chopped

Mash the ingredients together and arrange in a small bowl. Chill for 3 hours or more and serve with Melba toast. 'Special effects' can be obtained by making a batch of red and a batch of black and arranging them, half and half or in quarters, in the same dish. Suzanne O'Keeffe gave me this recipe.

Robert Cecil, the author, Marjory Davie
and Christopher Kininmonth with
Driver McCarthy, at Mycenae in 1946
(courtesy Mrs Patrick Leigh Fermor).

CHRISTOPHER'S PÂTÉ

I have happy memories of my late, and much lamented, friend,
the travel-writer, Christopher Kininmonth, refreshing himself
with draughts of ouzo while he made this in our Cyprus kitchen.
It could also be called Pâté Lorca, in honour of the famous line,
'Green, green, I want you green.' My wife, in a hurry to catch a
train, and stuck at red traffic-lights in a London taxi, once
declaimed this and the taxi-driver said, 'That's the Roy Campbell
translation, isn't it? Far the best.'

450g (1lb) leaf spinach
1 × 125g (4½oz) tin sardines
1 × 50g (2oz) tin anchovy fillets
100g (4oz) unsalted butter, at room temperature
a little ground black pepper
for garnish
1 hard-boiled egg, finely chopped

You cannot use tinned spinach in this recipe. You can use frozen spinach *en branche*, but not chopped or puréed. But I would strongly recommend that you use the fresh vegetable, particularly on grounds of colour.

Wash the spinach, and remove the stalks. Cook for about 3 minutes in 2 tablespoons of boiling salted water. Drain very thoroughly (I myself put the spinach in a colander and press it with a large clean stone, as I have already mentioned.) Drain and rinse the sardines and anchovy fillets. Put them, with the soft – but not melted – butter, the drained spinach and a little ground black pepper in a food processor. (A blender will do, though it is more difficult to get the thick paste out of the angles and off the little wheel.) Press the mixture into a very lightly oiled 450-ml (approximately ¾-pint) metal 'jelly mould'. Refrigerate for several hours. Turn out on to a plate and garnish with very finely chopped hard-boiled egg which, adhering to the sides of the small bright-green castle, creates a pleasing effect. Serve with hot toast.

Potted shellfish

It needn't just be shrimps. It can be prawns; it can be lobster; it can be crab. Whichever shellfish you pot, it will have been boiled, in saltwater or, ideally, in a *court-bouillon*. (Shellfish is the only kind of fish that is actually boiled – in the case of shrimps for only 4 minutes, and prawns for under 10.) Shrimps and prawns are potted whole. Lobster is cut into (small) 'bite-sized' pieces. The white crab meat you 'take as it comes', out of the shell.

200g (8oz) shelled shrimps, prawns, white crab meat *or* lobster pieces
juice of 1 lemon
a good pinch of salt
1 dessertspoon brandy
150g (6oz) best butter
cayenne pepper
½ teaspoon mace

Squeeze the lemon over the shellfish, and lightly season with salt. Warm the brandy in a small pan. Melt and heat 50g (2oz) of the butter in a pan with the cayenne and mace. Add the shellfish and the brandy, stirring all well together. Place in four small pots. Heat the rest of the butter, but do not allow it to boil. Pour it over the shellfish so that they are covered. Leave to cool before putting in the refrigerator (near the bottom). If you wish to keep the potted shellfish (they will keep for at least a week), cover with foil. Serve with hot toast, butter (for those who want it) and lemon quarters.

Fish salads

If one played that 'free association' game, beloved of psychoanalysts, with a selection of English people, and said, 'Salad', I am sure that ninety per cent would reply, 'Lettuce'. I am afraid that these respondents will be dissatisfied with the suggestions that follow, as not a single lettuce rears its head. I do not find a salad bowl lined with the coarse outer leaves attractive, and even the inner leaves seem to me to depend on dressing for their appeal. Nothing spoils and degrades a salad so quickly as lettuce, which acquires a bruised, beaten-up look and a slimy texture at remarkable speed. I really like only the tiny hearts, crunchy and yellow, lightly dressed with a little olive oil and lemon juice and sprinkled with a few chopped chives. (I am very fond of *cooked* cos lettuce: young, tightly packed specimens, simmered in herb stock for only 3 or 4 minutes, so that they remain still slightly crisp.) Even lettuce hearts (like beetroot) should be kept in solitary confinement on the salad table. So – lettuce-lovers, be warned.

RICE SALAD

Serves 6–8

This is one of my favourite cold first courses. I like to see (or, rather, to be one of) six congenial people seated round a table, helping themselves from the variegated, slightly glistening mound piled on a great dish in the centre.

675g (1½lb) cooked long-grain rice, still warm

250–300g (10–12oz) cooked fish of very good quality (lobster, scallops, crawfish, turbot, monkfish, John Dory, baby squid) cut into strips or large dice

1 green pepper, skinned, deseeded and cut into thin strips

1 red pepper, skinned, deseeded and cut into thin strips

1 medium Spanish onion, grated

Vinaigrette

---

6 tablespoons virgin olive oil

---

2 tablespoons good wine vinegar

---

1 generous teaspoon Grey Poupon or
other reliable Dijon mustard

---

2 cloves garlic, crushed

---

salt and pepper

---

for garnish

---

6 large unshelled cooked prawns

---

1 tablespoon finely chopped parsley

Rice slightly less than trebles in volume when cooked, so you will need to cook about 275g (10oz) according to the method on page 89. Meanwhile make the vinaigrette.

The unbreakable rule about vinaigrette is that it should consist of three parts oil to one part wine vinegar. This conceded, you can play about with seasonings. In this case, mix all the ingredients, except the oil, together. Then while whisking with a fork, gradually add the oil until the mixture is smooth and creamy.

Fork the vinaigrette thoroughly through the rice while it is still warm. Allow to cool. Shortly before serving, mix in the fish and other ingredients. (These can be varied: small capers and stoned black and/or green olives are a good addition.) The peppers should be skinned according to the method described on the page following before being deseeded and cut into strips.

Two-thirds rice to one-third of the other ingredients is usually recommended, but I say be generous with the fish. An excess of rice is the only fatal error. Pile the salad on a large platter (do not put it in a bowl). Sprinkle the mound with parsley and arrange the large prawns clinging to its sides. (By all means have more than six, but there must be at least one for each person.)

Stuffed vegetables

A rice salad of this kind (though the fish and peppers should be chopped smaller than they are here) can be used to stuff various vegetables, with pleasing effect.

Apricot-sized tomatoes should be opened at the stalk end, and very gently squeezed to expel the juice and seeds. With larger tomatoes you can use a pointed spoon to remove these and any white pith.

Cored courgettes should be very briefly cooked in olive oil.

Green, red and yellow peppers should be placed under a hot grill (or even held over a flame on a fork) to remove the skins. The blackened thin tough skin will flake off very easily, revealing the brilliant flesh underneath. (For some reason, a lot of people are intimidated by this idea: to them I say, 'Fear not!') Then slice the stalk end off the pepper and scrape out the seeds or pith.

In addition to filling tomatoes, courgettes and peppers with the rice mixture, it can also be rounded with a spoon on artichoke hearts. (These, in brine, are among the most bearable of tinned vegetables, if you can't be bothered to use the hearts of boiled fresh artichokes. Poach them for 2–3 minutes, though, in unsalted water, as they are rather too salty – and too tough.)

Note: Although I am very fond of stuffed aubergines, I would not recommend your stuffing them with fish; their own flavour is too strong.

Vegetables prepared as described above can also be stuffed with any minced fish bound with a well-seasoned mayonnaise (see page 31). Very finely chopped capers, raw or blanched onions, stoned olives, and so on can also be included.

Stuffed fruit

There are other possibilities. A friend of mind has a very whimsical way with lemons. He neatly cuts the tops off six fresh lemons and removes their contents. Discarding the pith, he mashes the juice and pulp with 120g (5oz) butter, a tin of drained rinsed sardines or tuna, a teaspoon of Dijon mustard, a good pinch of paprika and a sprinkling of freshly ground white pepper. With this mixture, he fills the lemon casings, which are then refrigerated. These lemons are served – their tops replaced – in egg-cups, and eaten with pointed egg-spoons.

Note: Despite the lavish provision of butter, this is a little too lemony for me. I would discard – or otherwise employ – the pulp and juice of two of the six lemons. Also, I never use white pepper (this is my particular cook's – as opposed to writer's – block).

Suddenly I imagine a great dish of mixed oranges and lemons. The removable cap of each is topped with a stalk and two green leaves. They would be filled with a mixture similar to the one described above. But what would I do with the insides of the oranges? Oranges go wonderfully with duck, with carrots, with strawberries, but the only fish they really seem to 'marry with' are red mullet. Perhaps I am imagining this dish just because it would look pretty and because I could name it 'The Belles of St Clement's'.

Stuffed eggs

Like almost everyone else I know, I have, in my time, mashed up the yolks of innumerable hard-boiled eggs with *Patum Peperium* or butter and crushed anchovies or anchovy essence, and used this as a filling for the whites. Now, at the thought, my eyelids – like Walter Pater's Mona Lisa's – are a little weary. I would far rather treat them as follows, with *Tapenade*.

TAPENADE

75g (3oz) anchovy fillets, rinsed and drained

300g (12oz) black olives, stoned

3 tablespoons capers, rinsed and drained

1 teaspoon Dijon mustard

½ teaspoon freshly ground black pepper

a pinch of allspice

1 tablespoon brandy

3 tablespoons pure virgin olive oil

Put all the ingredients in a food processor, except the olive oil, and process to a smooth paste. Transfer to a bowl, and gradually add the oil, as when making mayonnaise. (If you do not have a food processor, pound the solid ingredients and sieve them; then add the brandy, and finally the oil.)

The result is a delicious salty Mediterranean spread, very good on French bread, fresh or toasted. It can be used as a sauce for fish – cold or grilled – but not very subtle fish, such as sole or turbot, as it will overpower them. It can also be used to stuff eggs, as described below. (It will keep in the refrigerator for several weeks if you put it in a jar and cover it with a thin layer of olive oil.)

EGGS STUFFED WITH TAPENADE

hard-boiled eggs

1 recipe *Tapenade*

for garnish

finely chopped parsley

Cut the eggs in half lengthways. Remove the yolks and mash them with the *Tapenade*. Use about 1 dessertspoon per egg. The mixture should be solid enough to be rounded with a spoon when put into the hollow in the white. Sprinkle with parsley. (I would give each person 1½ or 2 eggs as a first course, with bread.)

Another way of serving this dish is simply to halve the eggs and cover them with the *Tapenade*, to which you will probably need to add a little extra olive oil. Garnish with parsley.

STUFFED MUSSELS

Despite its complexity, I highly recommend the Tokatlian recipe for Stuffed Mussels on page 147. Because it is served cold, it can be prepared in advance (though, I would admonish, on the same day as you are going to eat it, as it should not be refrigerated, only cooled).

There are many other simpler ways you can serve stuffed mussels, both hot (see page 208) and cold, as follows:

Open the mussels as directed in the Tokatlian recipe. (Personally I would advocate the steaming method, as I do not have the knack of opening them with a knife, which can lead to nasty injuries.) Remove the interior segment of beard. Pour the juices off the mussels and reduce them over a flame (or electric burner). Allow to cool. Now mix with a few spoonfuls of any cold sauce that appeals to you: Portobello Sauce (page 98), *Tapenade* (page 200), mayonnaise (page 31) flavoured according to your whim, vinaigrette (page 198), *Skordalia* (page 141). Pour the sauce over the mussels in the shells. A whole new world of adventure opens before you . . . Serve with fresh bread and butter.

Note: The Tokatlian recipe makes a very substantial starter. I would normally recommend it as a main dish, but, of course, as so often, simple reduction of quantity can turn a main dish into a first course.

SALADE NIÇOISE

I believe that food writers frequently attend conferences (though I have never been to one of these). Surely one must have been held in Nice (I wish I had been there) on the *Salade Niçoise*, about the contents of which there is unending debate.

In the past I have adopted a rather cavalier attitude to this salad, suggesting all sorts of innovations, both fishy and vegetable. But, with my recent intensified interest in simplicity, in 'the essentials', my aim is now to come as near as possible to the Platonic archetype of the *Niçoise*.

It is quite certain that the original *Niçoise* contained only raw vegetables. Let us begin, therefore, by omitting the cooked French beans or broad beans which are included in many recipes, and also the boiled potatoes. (I love potato salad, and fellow-devotees may regard the *Niçoise* as an excuse for enjoying a little of their treat. Make it separately, with a vinaigrette dressing; to me infinitely preferable, in the case of this salad, to one of mayonnaise.)

Now for the lettuce with which many people *line the bowl*. I would say that in Nice, this is omitted far more often than it is included. Whether you like lettuce or not, there are two good reasons for leaving it out: first, that it absorbs too much of the vinaigrette, and secondly that the glazed interior of a brown pottery bowl, or a plain white one, provides a background that sets off the brilliant colours of the salad far more effectively.

Cucumber is sometimes included. I have no objection to the presence of a small cucumber, peeled and thinly sliced.

Tinned tuna – or even fresh tunny home-preserved in oil – was not present in the original *Niçoise*. However, almost all recipes include it nowadays. One revered authority replaces it with tinned salmon. (Ugh!) I leave the decision to you, and certainly its inclusion makes the salad more substantial.

Note: Even the humblest grocery shops in Cyprus are stacked with tins of Japanese 'Light Meat' and 'White Meat' (the 'White Meat' is superior) tuna, canned – to me unsatisfactorily – in vegetable oil. I look forward to meeting it in its new form, canned in brine; not yet available here. Meanwhile I feel a great nostalgia for those great round tins of *tonno* in olive oil, from which one can buy a chunk of just the size one wants, in Italian provision shops such as the blesséd Olga Stores* in Islington.

What are we left with? Anchovy fillets, olives, tomatoes, onion, hard-boiled eggs and green peppers in a well-thought-out vinaigrette. Here is a salad which I think it would be difficult to improve on.

Note: This is one recipe in which you really must use real anchovies. Those 'anchovied fillets of sardine' simply will not do. If you cannot find real anchovy fillets in tins, buy the whole salted anchovies available from Greek, Italian and other foreign provision stores. These are packed in large round tins. You can buy any number of anchovies you wish. When you get them home, rinse off the salt with which they are encrusted. Then marinate them for several hours in olive oil and a little wine vinegar, with a clove of garlic. When you remove them from the marinade, they will skin and fillet easily from the tail upward. You will get four little fillets per fish.

10–12 anchovy fillets
100g (4oz) firm black olives, whole
8 large, ripe but firm tomatoes, quartered and then halved
1 medium-sized raw onion, cut into very thin rings
hard-boiled eggs, sliced into quarters, lengthways
2 green peppers, seeded and pithed, and cut into thin strips
1 small cucumber, peeled and thinly sliced
1 × 200g (7oz) tin tuna, flaked (optional)

*30 Penton Street, London N1 (tel. 01–837 5467).

Vinaigrette

6 tablespoons pure virgin olive oil
2 tablespoons red wine vinegar
1 clove garlic, crushed
1 teaspoon fresh basil leaves, finely chopped

The appearance of this salad is crucial. Arrange the ingredients with care in a plain bowl; there should be egg slices and anchovies near the top. Pour over the dressing. As with the Rice Salad on page 197, I like to put the bowl in the centre of the table and let people help themselves. Enough for six people without the tuna, and for eight if it is included.

Note: If you can get hold of really young, really tiny broad beans, do include 100g (4oz) of these, raw. Otherwise, if you don't feel the element of green in the salad is strong enough, scatter it with a few small green olives.

Other cold first courses

Finally, I should like to remind you of various other recipes in this book which make good cold first courses. (As I have already mentioned, the difference between a first course and a main course is often merely a matter of adjustment of quantities.) Try the Seafood Salad (page 120), the Squid Salad (page 135), the Island Marinated Fish (page 138), and Pickled Fish (page 143).

But . . .

Macbeth: What is that noise?
Seyton: It is the cry of women, my good lord.

And I can hear what they are crying: 'We want prawn cocktails.'

Shellfish cocktails

The prawn cocktail is served in some of the best and all the worst restaurants. Unfortunately I tend to associate it with the latter. My vision – I mean nightmare – is of frozen shrimps (sometimes not entirely thawed) or even tinned ones. They rest on lettuce cut into ribbons and intended to 'bulk out' the shrimps, and they are covered with bottled so-called mayonnaise, or even 'salad cream', tinted pink with tomato ketchup.

Waking, I wipe the sweat from my brow and remind myself that a shellfish cocktail need not be like this.

First of all, it need not be made of shrimps. (These usually masquerade as prawns in the cocktail of my nightmares.) It can be made of real prawns, of crab meat, of pieces of lobster, of cut-up, poached scallops, of just-opened oysters or mussels.

Allow 75–100g (3–4oz) shellfish per person. Marinate it in the vinaigrette given for Rice Salad (page 197) for at least an hour, then drain. Season enough mayonnaise (page 31) to coat the fish well with creamed horseradish and a drop or two of Tabasco. Colour pink, if you wish, with a little tomato juice. Fold the fish into this dressing. Spoon the mixture into glasses and garnish with watercress. In Cyprus, where watercress is not available I use *rocca* (rocket) which tastes very similar. (*Rocca* is obtainable in England from Cypriot greengrocers.)

Hot first courses

There are numerous recipes in this book which can be served as hot first courses. Once more – this is the last time, I promise – I reiterate that, with fish dishes, smaller quantities of main-course dishes make good first courses (and, very often, the reverse applies). See the recipes for Fried and Grilled Oysters (pages 13 and 14), for Whitebait (page 88), for Kedgeree (page 89), for Scallops and Bacon (page 92), the two recipes for Roes (page 104), for Mushrooms with Anchovy Cream (page 107), for Grilled

Fresh Sardines (page 111), for the two spaghetti dishes (pages 114 and 115), for Shrimp Risotto (page 117), for *Cod Florentine* (page 122), for *Sole Verdi* (page 125), for Island Marinated Fish (page 138) which can be served either hot or cold, for *Moules Marinière* (page 00), for Scallops *Meunière* (page 164), for Red Mullet in Wine (page 177), and for Cuttlefish Sausages (page 179).

However, I have one or two additional suggestions to make.

DEVILLED HERRINGS

I find few fish more delicious than a really fresh herring. Allow one herring for each person.

Score the cleaned herrings on each side. Spread them lightly with (made) English mustard and then sprinkle them with breadcrumbs. Put them under a heated grill for about 5 minutes on each side, basting with a little melted butter.

GRILLED TROUT

A small trout makes an excellent first course. Brush the cleaned trout with melted butter and put it under a hot grill, for 4–5 minutes on each side, basting with melted butter. Allow one trout per person.

The trout can be scattered with halved, blanched almonds, browned in melted butter, or it can be served with a pat of savoury butter on top of it. (In this case Parsley [also known as *Maître d'Hôtel*] Butter is ideal.)

Savoury butters are probably the simplest form of sauce. They are ideal with poached, fried or grilled fish. Parsley Butter is made by kneading 2 tablespoons of finely chopped parsley with 100g (4oz) softened butter. Season with a few drops of lemon juice and freshly ground pepper (also a pinch of salt if you are using unsalted butter). Refrigerate and put a pat on top of your fish.

207

The range of these butters is pretty well unlimited. Here are a few more examples, all of which follow the method for Parsley Butter, unless otherwise stated. (You omit the parsley, of course!)

For Anchovy Butter, pound three anchovy fillets to a paste and blend with the (unsalted in this case) butter, lemon juice and pepper. You can add a little grated onion. Do not add salt.

For Lumpfish Roe Butter, pound 1–2 tablespoons roe (the red looks prettier) with the other ingredients. Again, the butter should be unsalted, and you should not add salt.

For Garlic Butter, 3 cloves of garlic are pounded with 1 dessertspoon of parsley and 1 finely chopped shallot, before kneading with the butter and seasonings.

Lemon Butter is made by adding 1 teaspoon of finely grated lemon rind to the butter and seasonings.

For Mustard Butter, work 1 teaspoon of prepared (made) English mustard into the butter and seasonings. Add 1 teaspoon of finely chopped chives, if available. (If you had simply grilled your herring, above, instead of devilling it, Mustard Butter would have been an ideal accompaniment).

Orange Butter (made in the same way as Lemon Butter, with orange rind and orange juice substituted for lemon) is excellent with grilled red mullet.

Other ingredients for savoury butters are chives (see page 170), creamed horseradish, ground green peppercorns, purées (of raw celery, mushrooms, tomatoes, sweet peppers, black olives, capers). Have fun. This is a field in which any cook can use imagination and develop flair.

Savoury butters make ideal sauces for Hot Stuffed Mussels (see page 202 for cooking instructions). Having detached the inner portion of the beard, leave the mussels, with their juices, in the half-shell. Add a teaspoon of the savoury butter of your choice and put under a very hot grill for 1–2 minutes. Allow a dozen mussels for each person.

FILLETS OF
MACKEREL ANTIBOISE

As an alternative to using whole fish, you can make simple first
courses with fish fillets. I am fond of mackerel, but somehow it is
not my *beau idéal* of a first course, grilled whole. (You will have to
choose small fish, weighing about 225g (8oz), if you have a
preference for whole fish.) Accompany the fillets with Horseradish Butter or the traditional Gooseberry Sauce (450g (1lb)
unripe gooseberries, topped and tailed, boiled until soft in a little
water, drained and then puréed in the food processor/blender or
put through a sieve).

Serves 6, allowing 2 fillets per person

3 mackerel, each weighing about 300g
(12oz), cleaned and filleted (your
fishmonger will do this for you). Each
mackerel provides 4 fillets

a little flour,
seasoned with salt and pepper

100g (4oz) clarified butter (see page 167)

the white inner stalks of
1 head celery, chopped

the whites of 4 not-too-large leeks, chopped

4 skinned tomatoes, roughly chopped

a good pinch of salt and a sprinkling of
freshly ground black pepper

50g (2oz) *Beurre Noisette* (this is butter
cooked in a frying pan until it turns a
very pale brown, at which stage it has a
faint smell of nuts; hence its name)

a few drops of lemon juice

Lightly roll the mackerel fillets over a board spread with seasoned flour. Now in 50g (2oz) of the clarified butter, cook the celery and leeks until soft but not brown. Lightly fry the fillets of mackerel in the other 50g (2oz) of clarified butter. Keep warm in a serving dish at the bottom of a low oven. Now add the tomatoes to the celery and leeks. Heat the mixture (but do not cook sufficiently for the tomatoes to lose their fresh taste), adding salt and freshly ground black pepper. Pour this over the mackerel fillets. Make the *Beurre Noisette*, and add a few drops of lemon juice to it. Serve separately, with the dish of mackerel.

Coquilles

'Give me my scallop-shell of quiet,' wrote Sir Walter Raleigh. What he meant by this was that religious pilgrims used always to carry scallop-shells with them. I believe that this was originally something to do with St James of Compostela, whose shrine was a very popular destination for pilgrimages and after whom the French named the scallop *Coquille Saint-Jacques*. There is a story of a knight on horseback being miraculously converted to Christianity out at sea, through the influence of St James. When he emerged from the water, he and his horse were covered with scallop-shells ... I wish that, next time I go bathing, this would happen to me, for I find these shells wonderfully useful as containers for little hot first courses.

You can now get shells made of pyrex or of white ovenware, but to me this is not the same ... I want the real thing. When you buy scallops, demand from your fishmonger the deep-sided, concave upper shells. You can use them again and again, provided you clean them scrupulously each time. (When fish is served in these shells in restaurants where you feel faintly uneasy, study them with a piercing eye.)

Cooking in *coquilles* is a splendidly quick way of finishing off first courses you have prepared in advance. You will have already poached your fish (scallops themselves, or mussels; sole, monkfish, turbot or any firm white fish). With white fish you can include a few cooked shrimps or prawns. You can also use boiled crab meat or pieces of boiled lobster as the main ingredient. This is, of course, an excellent way of using up leftover fish (provided it is left over only from yesterday). I never seem to have any leftover fish, though my refrigerator is haunted by little saucers of cooked vegetables. You can use drained tinned salmon or tuna (not, of course, tinned oily fish such as anchovies or sardines) broken up into pieces, or flaked.

Start by lightly buttering your shell. Then put your fish in a sauce. Any of the *Béchamel*-based sauces is ideal. (There are three recipes for *Béchamel* in this book: my own on page 96, Mrs C. F. Leyel's on page 159 and Madame Prunier's on page 160. Take your pick!) To the *Béchamel*, you can add a third of its quantity of double cream to make a cream sauce, or you can add a pat of any type of savoury butter (see pages 207–8) to give it the flavour you desire. To make the classic onion sauce, *Sauce Soubise*, add three medium onions finely chopped and cooked until very soft in 50g (2oz) butter to 300ml (½ pint) *Béchamel*. (If you add 2 tablespoons of tomato purée and 1 dessertspoon of fresh, finely chopped basil to the *Soubise*, you will have a sumptuous tomato sauce.) Or add cheese to make the much-loved *Sauce Mornay* (see pages 161 and 162) . . .

The fish is in the sauce. The sauce is in the shell. Now comes the final stage: the topping. You can cover your sauced fish with mashed potatoes, lightly brushed with melted butter, or with breadcrumbs treated in the same way. Or, for a less filling first course, you can put a pat of savoury butter on top, or you can simply brush the top of the sauce itself with a little melted butter.

Meanwhile you have been heating up the grill. Now put your *coquilles* of fish under it. Remove them when they are heated through, and nicely brown on top.

Here, I have left many decisions up to you. Good cookery – and cookery that is satisfying to the cook – is a creative activity. As with every art, if it simply consists of following instructions, it will lack *joie de vivre* and 'zing'. Always present must be personal choice and a sense of adventure.

7
ENVOI – THE NUMINOUS QUALITY OF FISH

Numinous: divine; suggestive of divine presence or power. Discounting any connection between fish and my sudden glorious recovery from arthritis, it must nevertheless be said that there are magical and supra-normal qualities in fish, the most beautiful and mysterious of *zoa*.

Think only, for the moment, of the well-known life-cycles of the salmon and the eel, which display navigational skills beyond the capacity of the human brain to explain. For their size, too, fish are remarkably long-lived. That large herring you ate for breakfast is likely to be at least twenty years old. That fat plaice you paid so much for today at lunch is probably thirty or forty. Manifestly, fish carry within them factors which inhibit the early ageing process.

The extent of the rôle of shellfish, such as oysters, in the development of the brain in prehistoric man has not yet been gauged, but there is no doubt that that rôle was an important one in the development of what we call *Homo sapiens*.

The attitude to fish in the ancient world was a mixture of the sacred and the practical. Burkert in his fascinating book *Homo Necans* ('Man the Slaughterer') quotes an ancient Greek writer describing the customs of the Syrians:

'Every day the priests . . . bring to the goddess real fish and set it before her on a table, nicely cooked, both boiled and roasted, and then the priests of the goddess consume the fish themselves. For, according to Antipater of Tarsus, "Gatis the queen of the Syrians was such a gourmet that she issued a proclamation forbidding anyone to eat fish without Gatis." So, in fact the queen decreed "that no one might eat fish, but, rather, must bring it to her in the temple".'

In Babylon, 'catching and offering fish in the temple was a central act of piety without which no government could endure'.

The value placed on fish by the inhabitants of the ancient world was thus equally based on mysticism and gourmandise. As Burkert says: 'the coastal inhabitants around the Mediterranean sacralized the meal of fish itself'. The Greeks associated Aphrodite with the sea; and in the Ancient Roman pantheon of gods, fish were considered sacred to Venus, under whose protection they acquired the reputation of being symbols, and as food they were thought of as having aphrodisiac powers.

These attitudes to fish are by no means dead today. In her *Book of Middle Eastern Food*, Claudia Roden writes:

In some parts of the Middle East fish is still believed to have magical properties. Tunisians in particular believe it to be highly beneficial. The day after their wedding, couples are encouraged to step over a large fish as an assurance of happiness and a protection from evil. Today, the shape of a fish has become a symbol. Embroidered on material and carved in metal, it is believed to ward off the evil eye. In Egypt, one felt compelled to eat fish for the first meal in a new home. In Persia, fish is eaten on New Year's Day to cleanse the people from evil, while Jews display it in the centre of the Passover table as a symbol of fertility . . .

Also, of course, the shape of a fish was the symbol of the early Christians. Drawing it in the dust, they recognised that they were members of the same persecuted religion. Instead of being sacred to Venus, the fish had come to represent Christ. The word for fish, *ichthus*, stood for *Iesous Christos Theou Uios Soter* (Jesus Christ, Son of God, Saviour). In the 'quotes' which precede Izaak Walton's *Compleat Angler*, one otherwise unknown Henry Bayley writes, in Latin: 'There is one fish which is a doctor for the rest; for those to whom it is granted to touch that Doctor, health is assured. This is the wondrous exemplar of our Saviour Jesus, of whose name certain letters hold the mystery.'

Turning finally to the New Testament, what a part fishing plays in its narratives. Christ's disciples were fishermen who later became 'fishers of men'. When the disciples had 'toiled at their nets all night and taken nothing', Christ brought them a miraculous catch. 'And ... they filled both ships so that they began to sink' (Luke, chapter 5). When the multitude came to hear Christ preach, he produced the famous miracle of the loaves and 'a few little fishes' which became a feast (Matthew, chapter 14; Mark, chapter 8; Luke, chapter 9).

Finally, in John's account of a miraculous catch *after* the Resurrection (John, chapter 21), the disciples, 'as soon as they came to land, saw a fire of coals there, and fish laid thereon, and bread ... Jesus saith unto them, Come and dine ... and taketh bread, and giveth them, and fish likewise.'

BIBLIOGRAPHY

Eliza Acton, *Modern Cookery* (1845); see also *The Best of Eliza Acton*, ed. Elizabeth Ray, Penguin Books, Harmondsworth, 1986.

Soraya Antonius, *Simple Arab Cooking* (unpublished).

Mrs I. Beeton, *Book of Household Management* (1861) Ward Lock, London, 1987.

Mrs Beeton's Every-Day Cookery (1890) Ward Lock, London, 1982.

Ada Boni, *Talisman Italian Cook Book*, Pan Books, London, 1975.

Cape Cookery, 1890.

Elizabeth David, *An Omelette and a Glass of Wine*, Penguin Books, Harmondsworth, 1986.

Alan Davidson, *Mediterranean Seafood*, Penguin Books, Harmondsworth, 1987.

Arto der Haroutunian, *Middle Eastern Cookery*, Pan Books, London, 1982.

Lady Jekyll, *Kitchen Essays*, 1922.

Ruth Prawer Jhabvala, *Esmond in India*, John Murray, London, 1978.

Nancy Lake, *Menus Made Easy*, 9th edition 1899.

Mrs C. F. Leyel and Miss Olga Hartley, *The Gentle Art of Cookery* (1925), Chatto & Windus, London, 1970.

Theoni Mark, *Greek Island Cooking*, Batsford, London, 1978.

Vicomte de Mauduit, *The Vicomte in the Kitchen*, James Clarke & Co Ltd., London, 1933.

Prosper Montagne, *Larousse Gastronomique*, Paul Hamlyn, London, 1988.

Madame Prunier's Fish Cookery Book (1938), trans. and ed. Ambrose Heath, Hutchinson, London, 1972.

Claudia Roden, *Mediterranean Cookery*, BBC Enterprises, London, 1987.

Claudia Roden, *A Book of Middle Eastern Food*, Thomas Nelson, London, 1968; revised edition Penguin Books, Harmondsworth, 1986.

Mrs de Salis, *Savouries à la Mode*, 1896.

Constance Spry and Rosemary Hume, *The Constance Spry Cookery Book* (1956), Dent, London, 1978.

Flora Thompson, *Lark Rise to Candleford* (1945), Penguin Books, Harmondsworth, 1973.

Victory Cookbook, Cape Town, 1940s.

Izaac Walton, *The Compleat Angler* (1653), The World's Classics, Oxford University Press, 1982.

Florence White, *Good Things in England*, Jonathan Cape, London, 1932.

INDEX

aubergines:
  ratatouille, 168
avgolemono, salsa, 140
avgolemono psarasoupa, 176–7
avgotarakho, 191
avocado:
  Portobello sauce, 98–9

Babylon, 213
bacon:
  angels on horseback, 102–3
  baked white fish, bacon and
    green peas, 93
  fish with bacon, 92
  scallops and bacon, 92–3
baked white fish, bacon and green
    peas, 93
Balliol College, Oxford, 18
barbounia krasata, 177–8
Barry, Sir Charles, 28
basil:
  pesto, 127–8
bass *see* sea-bass
Bayley, Henry, 214
BBC, 18, 81
Béchamel, Marquis de, 161
Béchamel sauce, 96–7, 108, 161,
    163, 211
Beeton, Mrs, 12, 24, 100–1
Bernhardt, Sarah, 171, 173
Bertorelli's, Charlotte Street, 110
beurre noisette, 209
Bible, 214
Bingham, Mrs, 3, 5–6
Bloom, Leonard, 144
Bloom's Baroque pickled fish,
    145–6
boiling, 150
Boni, Ada, 116
Bower, Leonard, 19
bread:
  skordalia, 141
  tarator sauce, 151

bream:
  samak bi tahina, 156
  samak harra, 157–8
  sea-bream with red wine, 67
Briand, M., 88
brill Italienne, 61
Brillat-Savarin, Anthelme, 101
broad beans:
  salade Niçoise, 205
brodetto, 111–12
Brown, James, 78
Buchan, John, 12
Buller (college porter), 78, 79
Burgundy, 159
Burkert, 213
Burnham Beeches, 10–11
butter:
  anchovy, 208
  beurre noisette, 209
  chive, 170
  clarified, 167
  garlic, 208
  lemon, 208
  lumpfish roe, 208
  mustard, 208
  orange, 208
  parsley, 207

Café de Paris, London, 81
Café Royal, London, 81
Cairo, 18, 27–8
calcium, 41
calories, 42
Campbell, Mrs Patrick, 171, 173
Campbell, Roy, 194
canapés à la Prince de Galles, 102
Cape Town, 142–4
capers:
  halibut with capers and olives,
    53
  salmon with dill and capers, 47
  tapenade, 200–1
Cavendish, Milla, 173

tunny fish *see* tuna
turbot:
  fritto misto, 118–20
  sayyadieh, 154–5
  turbot with fennel root and
    sweet peppers, 46
Turkish cooking, 146–53
Turville-Petre, Francis, 2, 19–26,
  128–9
Twelve Crows Nest, 10

Vatel, 159
vegetables, stuffed, 199
Venus, 213
vinaigrette, 198, 205
vitamin A, 41–2
vitamin D, 41–2
Voltaire, 96

Waller, Fats, 81–2
walnuts:
  hamsi tavasi, 152–3
  midya litsk, 147–8

  samak harra, 157–8
  tarator sauce, 151
Walton, Izaak, 11–12, 214
Waugh, Evelyn, 19
Wheeler's, 79
White, Florence, 93, 106, 107
white fish flan, 94–5
whitebait, 88
  fritto misto, 118–20
  psaria marinata, 138–9
whiting:
  avgolemono psarasoupa, 176–7
  sayyadieh, 154–5
Wilkinson, Colonel, 34
Williams, Spencer, 80, 81–2
wine:
  barbounia krasata, 177–8
  sea-bream with red wine, 67
Woolley, Frank, 37, 84–5
Worcester College, Oxford, 11,
  12, 16, 76–9

Yianni, 25, 26

227